Dedicated to my beautiful little princess ... Aaliyah

Easy Indian SuperMeals

for babies, toddlers and the family

by

Zainab Jagot Ahmed

www.ZainabJagotAhmed.com

Published by Sweet Juicy Lime 2014

Text © Zainab Jagot Ahmed 2014

Photographs and design © Zainab Jagot Ahmed 2014 and © Sweet Juicy Lime 2014

Cover photography © Photoshootr 2014

Design layout DeCiacco Design

British Library Cataloguing-in Publication Data

A catalogue record for this book is available on request from the British Library

ISBN: 978-0-9929643-0-6

Printed in England

This book provides information that is for educational purposes only, and all views and advice expressed are those of the author based on first-hand parenting experience. It should not under any circumstance take the place of professional nutritional or medical advice. Please talk to your health care providers (doctors, health care visitors) if you are unsure about using spices in baby food, have any questions about specific foods, food allergies, or require further advice about any of the information in this book.

Whilst every effort has been made to ensure the contents of this book is accurate, reliable and safe, the author or publisher cannot be held responsible for any damages arising from the use of the information in this book. If your child is ill or appears to be suffering from an allergic reaction, please consult with your doctor or relevant healthcare professional immediately.

Contents

Introduction

Every parent wants to feed their baby nutritious food to ensure their little one has the best start in life. So being a new mum, I was extremely cautious about the types of food I was feeding my daughter Aaliyah, when I began weaning her at 6 months. Which I'm sure every woman can relate to at some point during her career as 'mum'.

After reading books, numerous websites, and seeking advice from family and friends about weaning and the best weaning foods, my anxiety about "where to begin?!" settled, and Aaliyah's solid food journey began. I started with iron-fortified baby rice (with her usual milk), and pureed fruit and vegetables combined with her regular milk feeds. That seemed straight forward enough. However, only a month later when Aaliyah turned 7 months old, she was already set for Stage 2 feeding (soft lumps, new tastes, flavours and textures). The confusion and panic of "what should I feed her now?!" started all over again! Buying bland, processed, lumpy baby food was not appealing in the slightest! Particularly as the more processed the food, the more additives it contains which ultimately means the nutritional content is reduced.

I completely understand how tempting it is to buy processed baby food if you are a frantic busy parent, and it is fine occasionally, but feeding your little one nutritionally inadequate food will be detrimental to health, as babies need nutrient-rich food for healthy growth.

Similarly it is vital to shape healthy eating habits as early as possible and to maintain these habits, to help control the obesity crisis currently affecting the UK. With one in three children in England (33.3%) being either overweight or obese in their final year of primary school (Year 6), along with over a fifth (22.2%) of 4-5 year olds (source: National Child Measurement Programme 2012/13); it is imperative to act now as obese children are increasingly likely to grow into obese adults. Potentially leading to diabetes, high blood pressure and joint problems later in life. For obese children there are additional psychological effects such as low self-esteem if they are teased and bullied at school.

Therefore home-cooking was the obvious choice for me because I could cook with nutrient-rich foods and know exactly what ingredients were going into Aaliyah's meals. It would be cost-effective, fresh, healthy and tastier. By planning ahead I could also cook and freeze meals for the forthcoming week, saving valuable time too.

So Aaliyah's Stage 2 feeding began with steamed vegetables and cheese all blended to a soft lumpy consistency. But then I thought, "why am I feeding my daughter such bland food?" Being a British Asian, I wasn't raised on steamed veggies and cheese and neither are billions of other people across the world!

Wanting Aaliyah to be in touch with her roots, I searched for Indian-influenced baby food recipes online and for any cookery books I could buy, but surprisingly I didn't find much. I also asked family and friends if they knew of any good Indian baby food cookery books, and they didn't know of any either. We were all in the same boat! One day, deep in thought I felt a flicker of inspiration and then 'PING!'... light bulb moment! I decided to create my own healthy adaptations of traditional Indian recipes.

My first attempt was Gajar Halwa (carrot dessert), simply because the main ingredient is carrot, a very tasty sweet root vegetable which is extremely healthy for babies. I cooked up a batch following a conventional recipe but stripped it right back to remove all the bad stuff. I avoided overcooking the carrots as some recipes suggest, maintaining their moisture and natural sweetness, and the sugar was replaced with raisins. I served it up to my daughter and SUCCESS! Her little eyes lit up with delight after the first mouthful as though it was her first trip to a sweet shop, she wanted more and more. Then suddenly 'PING!'... light bulb moment! I thought "WOW, she loved it! I'm going to write an Indian-inspired baby and toddler food cookery book!"

After the success of this recipe I spent a period of months researching and detailing the health benefits of culinary spices, also known as **'SuperSpices'**, **food groups** and **'SuperFoods'**, to ensure I provided Aaliyah with all of the vitamins and minerals she needed for healthy growth and development. After collating this information, I experienced yet another light bulb moment and came up with the concept of creating 'SuperMeals' for babies, toddlers and the whole family. So that my fellow mummy is the story of how this book came to be.

What are 'SuperMeals'?

The 'Super' of SuperMeals refers to the extra health benefits associated with these meals over and above normal meals, due to the inclusion of carefully selected foods, SuperFoods and SuperSpices. When fused together they produce scrumptious meals chock-full with nutritional value for babies and toddlers. In other words:

Regular Foods
+ SuperFoods
+ SuperSpices
= SuperMeals

I've used my 'Banana and Cinnamon Roti Wrap' recipe, as an example of how SuperMeals work in this cookery book:

Roti (Regular Food)
+ Banana (SuperFood)
+ Cinnamon (SuperSpice)
= Roti Wrap (SuperMeal)

The roti (Indian flatbread or chapatti) fulfils the basic starchy food requirement to provide much-needed energy for baby; the banana, an excellent high-energy fruit provides potassium vital for heart function, healthy muscle growth and helps the body to absorb calcium; the cinnamon contributes towards a healthy immune system, is great for digestion and brain function, as well as offers a warm fragrant sweetness. All of these

health benefits wrapped up into one tasty snack that your little one will wholeheartedly munch on. So you can rest assured I have created some cracking recipes that are **delicious, powerful, energy-packed, well-balanced SuperMeals**, boosting the antioxidant levels on your little one's colourful plastic plate.

Who is this Book For?

Easy Indian SuperMeals for babies, toddlers and the family, is a useful culinary guide for any parents looking to ditch the bland baby food, to move on to yummy, adventurous baby food. Expectant mums (for future reference), new mums, existing parents who want to try something a bit different with their second, third or fourth child, or anyone interested in Indian -inspired, aromatic baby food.

It is essentially for any parents who not only want to provide their little ones with tasty wholesome meals, they are also interested in learning about the health benefits of foods and aromatic spices for baby and the rest of the family; making Easy Indian SuperMeals for babies, toddlers and the family a handy reference guide for years to come.

How this Book Works

Initially all vegetarian, meat, fish, dessert recipes (and so on) all have their own dedicated chapters. Purely because in the early stages of feeding, babies' requirements are very specific. So I have included all the 'specifics' at the beginning of each chapter along with some of my personal experiences of introducing these meals to Aaliyah. As I wanted to share these experiences with you to ease any concerns you may have and offer other useful advice.

The earlier chapters are also formatted in this manner for convenience. For busy parents who want to find the fish or vegetarian recipes quickly, to ensure their little one is receiving a balanced diet, for parents who may have specific dietary requirements they wish to pass onto their little one i.e. vegetarianism; or parents simply looking for the dessert chapter for a scrummy treat. For these reasons you'll notice that Stage 2 and Stage 3 recipes can be found alongside each other within these chapters.

As your little one progresses on to Stage 4: 1-3 Years recipes, toddlers can eat pretty much everything and the specifics begin to diminish. For this reason all vegetarian, meat and fish meals are under the same chapter but are all clearly labelled for convenience.

And finally, as your little one moves in to the school years (3 years plus), there's a handy chapter at the end of this book focussed solely on preparing quick, tasty meals for kids – all meals ready in 15 minutes or less.

By the way, throughout this book baby is referred to as 'she'. There is no reason for this other than I have a daughter as you know, so for me it was the obvious choice.

Feeding Stages

Recipes are suitable for **weaning babies aged from 7 months onwards**. There are no recipes aimed at Stage 1 (6 months plus) weaning babies simply because spices are not suitable for babies of this age. The feeding stages within this book include:

Stage 2 - 7 Months Plus: babies ready for new textures, soft lumps, new tastes and new flavours, by introducing tiny amounts of aromatic spices to tempt curious little taste buds. Self-feeding also begins.

Stage 3 - 10 Months Plus: older babies ready to progress to the next level of spice for more flavoursome meals. Meals are chunkier consisting of chopped food instead of mashed. Self-feeding continues.

Stage 4 - 1-3 Years Plus: spice training complete. Toddlers ready for family meals with some small changes.

The School Years – 3-5 Years Plus: pre-schoolers and older school children needing quick, tasty nutritious meals to satisfy hunger pangs after a busy day at school.

Please note: feeding stages are loose guidelines and should not be referred to as strict timeframes for recipe usage, as recipes can be adapted to reflect the relevant feeding stage of your little one. For example, I was feeding Aaliyah Stage 2 and Stage 3 SuperMeals when she was 10 months old, by simply increasing the level of spice in my Stage 2 recipes to reflect that of Stage 3. So a quarter teaspoon of garlic was increased to half a teaspoon or even one teaspoon, whilst following the same recipe.

I also left the food chunkier and served curries with accompaniments such as rice, roti, pitta bread and quinoa to make the meals more filling. I personally found this worked really well as Aaliyah had quite a few favourite meals in the Stage 2 recipes, so this enabled her to enjoy them for longer.

IMPORTANT: do not feed your little one any recipes earlier than the recommended start age.

Cooking Technique

The method in which most of these recipes are prepared differs from conventional Indian cooking in that not everything is always thrown in the same pot to bubble away until tender. I altered my cooking technique accordingly to ensure I maintained as many nutrients as possible when cooking fruit and vegetables. Therefore you'll notice within many recipes the fruit and vegetables are steamed separately and added to the meal at the end.

About the Recipes - No-added Salt, Sugar or Chillies!

Choose from yummy vegetable, meat or fish curries, desserts and finger foods as your little one graduates from one feeding stage and onto the next. Some are **traditional Indian recipes with a twist** such as my scrumptious 'Sweet Potato, Apple and Dhal Curry'. Others are inspired by World cuisine but with an Indian twist, such as my mouth-watering 'Indian Vegetable Paella', 'Playdate Pizza Pitta Fingers' and a twist on the British classic 'Desi Mac 'n' Cheese with Tuna'; all guaranteed to leave your little one with a very full and satisfied tummy.

Feeding Baby New Meals - What to Expect

I know how exciting (and also frustrating) offering new meals to baby can be. Enthusiastically I'd cook up a storm in the kitchen and when Aaliyah's meal was ready, I'd put her in her high chair (armed with bib), spoon-feed her her first mouthful, and wait in anticipation for her response; like a contestant on Master Chef waiting for the judge's approval.

In my experience I found her initial responses to be quite extreme. She either loved her meal straight away gobbling up the whole bowl, or she'd push the food out with her tongue. When she did this I felt really disheartened, thinking 'oh no, what if I'm a terrible cook and she can't tell me!'

As time went on, I realised although she appeared not to enjoy some meals, when I offered them to her again either later the same day or another day, she happily devoured the whole bowl. As she had already experienced the initial taste, the taste and texture was not a surprise to her anymore.

Now Aaliyah eats almost everything and loves her food which is great for family meal time and for holidays away from home. In fact, she is very enthusiastic about trying new types of food which is amazing and a huge relief for me. I like to think in her mind:

food from mummy = yummy food for me to eat

So stay strong and persevere! If your little one seems to reject the meals you have prepared either using your own recipes, or from using recipes in this cookery book; offer the meals again at another time as she may develop a taste for it later, whether it be a week or months' time.

Following the food spitting, turning away from food and spoon pushing, rest assured all recipes have now been approved and awarded gold stars by my little Princess Aaliyah, and her little friends - the toughest of all food critics.

SuperSpices

'SuperSpices', although have been used for medicinal purposes and general well-being across different cultures for generations, is a term recently awarded to culinary spices by researchers due to their remarkable health promoting properties and potent antioxidant levels. A concept recently supported by the U.S. Department of Agriculture (USDA). After examining antioxidant activity of specific foods, fruit, vegetables and spices amongst others, they found culinary spices such as cloves, cinnamon and turmeric are bursting with powerful antioxidants. Antioxidants that have an even higher level than some of the more popular SuperFoods such as blueberries and avocados, as you'll see in the below pyramid.

Antioxidant Levels - SuperSpices vs SuperFoods

Vertical axis: Antioxidant Levels (Low → High)

Legend: SuperSpices / SuperFoods

				Cloves, ground				
			Oregano, dried	Rosemary, dried	Thyme, dried		SuperSpices	
			Cinnamon, ground	Turmeric, ground	Vanilla beans, dried		SuperFoods	
			Sage, ground	Parsley, dried	Nutmeg, ground			
		Basil, dried	Cumin, seed	Curry powder	White pepper	Ginger, ground		
		Black pepper	Chilli powder	Paprika	Black raspberries	Ginger root		
	Golden raisins	Prunes	Garlic powder	Red plums	Blackberries	Garlic, fresh	Coriander, fresh	
	Blueberries	Dill, fresh	Strawberries	Dates, deglet noor	Cherries	Cardamom	Apples	
	Asparagus	Green pears	Oranges	Red-fleshed guava	Avocados	Peaches	Red grapes	
Beets	Black grapes	Pink/red grapefruit	Green leaf lettuce	Spinach	Broccoli	Lemons	Mangoes	Apricots
White potatoes	Aubergine (eggplant)	Sweet potatoes	Cauliflower	White onion	Red bell pepper	Banana	Carrots	Tinned tomatoes
White mushrooms	Green peas, frozen	Cabbage	Pumpkin	Squash	Tomato	Cantaloupe melon	Papaya	Watermelon

Adapted from: USDA Database for the Oxygen Radical Absorbance Capacity (ORAC) of Selected Foods, Release 2.

NOTES:
- Fruit and vegetables towards the bottom of the pyramid are still SuperFoods therefore will contain a higher level of nutrients over regular foods.
- Does not represent the entire list of foods within the report. Only the most popular SuperFoods have been selected for comparison purposes.
- Further research is underway to determine whether and how SuperSpice antioxidant levels benefit human health.

Consuming antioxidants is massively important for our health to protect our bodies against free radical cell damage. Free radicals are unstable, highly reactive molecules triggered by pollution, pesticides in food, alcohol, smoking and excess fat consumption; causing serious diseases such as heart disease, cancer, strokes, Alzheimer's disease and arthritis later in life.

SuperSpices also possess anti-inflammatory properties which protect us from infections, allergies, asthma and more. In fact research has shown holy basil has anti-inflammatory action comparable to the common painkiller Ibuprofen. And more recently, carvacrol, a plant compound found in Oregano is believed to be effective against the infectious winter vomiting bug, the norovirus. Offering yet another reason why spices have been awarded with their SuperSpice status.

SuperSpices in Baby Food - The 'Official' View

Using Indian spices in baby food seems to be a relatively new subject at the moment. There's an abundance of 'official' advice available through the internet, books and health care services focussing on introducing solid food to babies. A great starting point but official rulebooks mostly ignore the use of aromatic spices in home-cooked baby food. If it is not included in the official advice this doesn't imply that you cannot use spices in baby food. It is important to remember these are only recommendations and guidelines. There are no solid procedures you must follow as a parent. So go ahead and throw out the rulebook! You know your baby best so go with what feels right for you and your little one.

Nevertheless, as the popularity of Indian and exotic baby food grows, attitudes towards using Indian spices are changing, and the fact that the differences are cultural rather than based on scientific findings is coming to the forefront. Being a British Asian I have both Indian and English culture under my belt, and I can tell you from first-hand experience the difference is entirely cultural. As a child, my mum fed me and my sister's delicious, flavoursome curries with roti and rice from a very young age. This was the first food I ate even before I was introduced to simple foods like sandwiches when I started school.

Feeding Baby SuperSpices - A Good Idea?

Absolutely! Despite the fact research is currently on-going to understand exactly if and how the antioxidant levels in SuperSpices works to improve health, they do possess a number of other distinct advantages. Some of which I will explore now.

Creates aromatic, tasty baby food: Our sense of taste and smell are very closely linked. So much so, that food would taste bland without our sense of smell. Spices release a delicious aroma when cooked making the food tastier when eaten. A wonderful alternative to adding salt and sugar into baby's food. They will help you create incredibly tasty meals that your little one will whole heartedly enjoy.

Wider variety of meals: Spices are extremely versatile! Changing one spice in a dish will alter the taste completely. This versatility suggests you can offer a wider variety of meals to your little one. More variety in your little ones diet now, will help to keep a fussy eater at bay later. So put the bland food away, and start spicing up that baby food!

Family meal training: If your family meals are already full of flavour, introducing aromatic spices in small amounts gradually will be milder on her little tummy, rather than going from zero to 100 percent in one go. Great spice preparation for the big family meals that await her.

Unique health benefits: Each SuperSpice has its own unique health benefits all members of the family can take advantage of. I have outlined the advantages for the core spices I use in my recipes so you can see how beneficial spices will be in your little ones diet.

Black Pepper: Helps to settle indigestion, constipation and reduces pain in toothaches.

Cardamom: Prevents cold and flu (influenza), flatulence and throat infections. Also treats asthma, bronchitis and analgesic properties treat teeth and gums.

Cinnamon: Aids digestion, treats diarrhoea, strengthens the immune system to cure colds, boosts memory and cognitive function, balances blood sugar level (type 2 diabetes) and analgesic properties help to reduce pain in toothaches.

Cloves: Antiseptic properties help fight against colds and flu, bronchitis and athletes foot. Treats flatulence and boosts memory, digestion and blood circulation. Analgesic properties reduce pain in toothaches.

Coriander: Aids digestion, treats diarrhoea, provides iron helping to prevent anaemia and protects the skin against eczema and dryness.

Cumin: Supports the development of a healthy immune system, improves oxygen distribution, betters digestion, boost metabolism and improves the absorption of nutrients.

Paprika: Antibiotic properties help protect against bacterial infections such as tonsillitis, improves blood circulation and aids digestion.

Turmeric: Antibacterial properties help prevent infection in wounds and cuts, aids digestion, boosts immune system function for cold and flu protection, and reduces flatulence and the risk of childhood leukaemia developing.

'Super-Spicy' breast milk: And finally, did you know if you have been or are currently breastfeeding your little one, she will already have tasted the foods and spices you have been eating. Subtle tastes pass through breast milk and straight into baby's tummy. As spices are already a familiar taste, why not add a pinch of aromatic spices in with her solid food?

Which SuperSpices are Safe to Use in Baby Food?

Most are safe to use in baby's diet in fresh, ground or dried varieties, provided they are introduced in the correct manner (see How Should I Introduce SuperSpices to Baby?).

Below is an idea of the aromatic spices you can introduce although there are more, including chilli powder! Feel free to experiment with them (and others) to uncover new and exciting meals for baby.

When is it Safe to Introduce SuperSpices to Baby?

From 7 to 8 months of age, when your little one is comfortable eating basic solid food i.e. fruits, vegetables. Through personal experience, I introduced aromatic spices into Aaliyah's diet from 7 months of age. I had no problems and she absolutely loved her food, eating all of her meals with gusto.

How Should I Introduce SuperSpices to Baby?

Firstly, follow the 'four day rule' to ensure your little one is not allergic to new spices you have introduced i.e. introduce a spice cooked within food, and wait four days before introducing another one to ensure there are no allergic reactions. I did this by lightly cooking the spice in olive oil and adding it to freshly cooked mashed potato.

SuperSpices Safe to Use in Baby Food

Basil	Garlic powder	Pepper (black & white)
Cardamom	Ginger (ground)	Rosemary
Cinnamon	Mint	Saffron
Cloves	Nutmeg	Sage
Coriander	Oregano	Thyme
Cumin	Paprika	Turmeric
Dill	Parsley	Vanilla

Whilst allergic reactions to spices are uncommon, they can occur. So keep an eye out for tummy upsets, skin rashes, swelling of the lips and face, runny and blocked noses, sneezing, itchy watery eyes, nausea, vomiting and diarrhoea. Please be particularly cautious if you have a family history of allergic reactions to specific spices.

Secondly, introduce spices using just a pinch at a time. All of my recipes suitable for Stage 2-7 Months Plus babies are created with this in mind. The food may taste bland to you and I, but a pinch really is enough at this stage. It's amazing what new taste buds can detect!

Please feel free to consult with your doctor or health visitor before introducing new spices into your little ones diet.

SuperFoods & Food Groups

So we've discovered SuperSpices are a fantastic edition to your little ones meals for enhancing taste and for her general health. However, we must not forget to look at major food groups SuperSpices should be consumed with in order to gain optimal health benefits at mealtimes.

All foods contain some nutritional value which will be beneficial to baby, however, there are other foods naturally chock-full with an even HIGHER amount of nutrients. These foods have been labelled 'SuperFoods', as they are known to have extra health benefits. As with SuperSpices they contain antioxidants, however, these antioxidants have been scientifically proven to benefit health, making them hugely important for baby's well-being and for fighting off diseases. So SuperFoods are the healthy start all babies need and can be found within every food group.

Food Groups - Getting the Balance Right for Baby

Estimated Average Requirements (EAR) for Energy:

7 to 9 months:	boys	825kcal per day
	girls	765kcal per day
10 to 12 months:	boys	920kcal per day
	girls	865kcal per day

(Source: Department of Health, Dietary Reference values for Food Energy and Nutrients for the UK)

Between the ages of 8 and 9 months, your little ones diet should consist of three balanced meals a day. As she grows and requires more energy, this should gradually increase to three balanced meals and two healthy snacks per day.

There are four major food groups outlined below baby must consume from to attain her recommended calorie intake, and to achieve a balanced diet. A balanced diet ensures your little one gets all of the vitamins and minerals she needs to grow into a healthy adult.

Food Groups	Baby's Serving Size (per day)
Carb-Rich (Starches)	3-4 servings
Fruit and Vegetables	3-4 servings
Milk and Dairy Foods	3 servings
Protein-Rich	1-2 servings

Carb-Rich (Starches)

Being one of the largest food groups also makes it one of the most important. Bread, rice, potatoes, pasta, fortified breakfast cereals, rice, roti's and cous cous are all included under the starchy foods umbrella. Providing your little one with valuable nutrients, fibre and much-needed energy to crawl, walk and play. Potatoes are not classed as a vegetable portion due to their high starch content. So if you do feed your little one potato, include some other vegetables along with her meal.

From 9 months onwards feed your little one, three to four servings of starchy foods per day.

Carb-Rich SuperFood: Whole Grains

Whole grains such as wholemeal bread, whole wheat pasta, brown rice and wholemeal cereals are the SuperFoods of this group. They are antioxidant, anti-cancer, keep the heart healthy, and are high in fibre and in complex carbohydrates. Complex carbohydrates break down to produce glucose (a type of sugar), and when transported around the body via the blood stream is transformed into energy.

Although whole grain varieties are nutritionally better, feeding your little one too many high fibre foods can stop the absorption of important minerals such as iron and calcium. Potentially leading to anaemia later in life and affecting mental and physical growth. They can also fill up your little ones tummy before she's eaten the necessary amount of calories required for healthy growth. With both points in mind, I opted to feed Aaliyah a combination of white and whole grain varieties of starchy foods, as they both contain complex carbohydrates.

Fruit and Vegetables

Nature has provided us with a vast array of delicious and colourful fruit and vegetables, each containing unique vitamins, minerals and fibre essential to our health. So being another large food group, feel free to go fruit and veg crazy because this group is bursting at the seams with SuperFoods. So take advantage of these natural sources and feed your little one a rainbow of as many different coloured fruit and vegetables as you can, to ensure you are giving your little one a balanced diet. Fruit and vegetables don't always need to be fresh; give them a try in dried, canned or frozen varieties.

Feed your little one fruit and vegetables in each meal, three to four servings per day.

Fruit and Vegetable SuperFoods: The Rainbow

Red	Cherries, grapes, guava, papaya, raspberries, red bell pepper, red/pink grapefruit, strawberries, tomatoes, watermelon.
Yellow / Orange	Apricots, cantaloupe melons, carrots, lemons, mangoes, oranges, peaches, pumpkins, squash, sweet potatoes.
Green	Asparagus, avocados, broccoli, cabbage, kale, lettuce, peas, spinach, watercress.
Blue / Purple	Aubergine, beets, blackberries, blueberries, grapes, plums, prunes, raisins, raspberries.
White	Apples, bananas, cauliflower, garlic, ginger, mushrooms, onions, potatoes.

Red

Lycopene is a nutrient and part of the carotenoid family, a group of naturally occurring plant pigments. Therefore the crimson and vibrant pillar box red colour of certain fruit and vegetables, can be attributed to this carotenoid.

Lycopene, currently one of the most powerful antioxidants in food is believed to help prevent heart disease and reduce several types of cancer. The most concentrated source is found in tomatoes. However, the tomatoes must be cooked in order for the body to absorb lycopene more efficiently. Great news as Indian cuisine involves heavy usage of tomatoes when cooking curries. Used in fresh, pureed or tinned varieties, all of which when cooked are great sources of lycopene for your little one.

It is also worth knowing tinned tomatoes contain an even higher antioxidant level than fresh, cooked tomatoes! So there's no need to feel guilty about grabbing a tin of chopped tomatoes from the cupboard if you're short for time, it will actually be better for your family's health. Just be aware excess consumption of lycopene, although harmless, can lead to a yellow liver and skin!

Lycopene, although found in small quantities is also present in numerous SuperSpices such as chilli powder, paprika, cinnamon, black pepper, oregano, garlic powder and curry powder.

Orange and Yellow

Beta-carotene, one of the most popular carotenoids is responsible for the orange and yellow pigment found in particular fruit and vegetables. Beta-carotene is important for baby for its antioxidant and anti-cancer properties. It also has fabulous anti-ageing properties for us mums! When consumed, it is converted into vitamin A. Vitamin A is essential for healthy vision and skin, and for boosting immune system function to protect against cold and flu viruses.

Beta-carotene is also found in less 'orange' vegetables such as spinach and red leaf lettuce. As with lycopene, beta-carotene can too be found in SuperSpices: dried basil, parsley, oregano, sage and ground coriander.

Citrus fruits - oranges and lemons are an excellent concentrated source of vitamin C, rather than vitamin A. Vitamin C is antioxidant and although doesn't cure the common cold, prevents further complications such as pneumonia from occurring.

Green

Although coloured by the plant pigment 'chlorophyll', it's the carotenoids lutein and zeaxanthin found in the green group that are beneficial to health. Lutein and zeaxanthin are antioxidant and generally found in dark leafy green vegetables. They are also found in less 'green' places such as egg yolks, grapes, corn and in different varieties of squash. A diet rich in lutein and zeaxanthin can keep eyes healthy, leading to a reduced risk of cataracts later in life.

Green vegetables, and other vegetables from the cruciferous family (broccoli, cabbage and cauliflower), are linked to research suggesting they are anti-cancer and high in vitamins A, C and B vitamins such as folate.

Folate, and other B vitamins, are necessary for the production of red blood cells and are essential for converting food into energy, which your little one will need for running around. Folate in particular, is also important for producing and maintaining new cells which is essential for healthy growth during infancy.

Blue and Purple

Coloured by the plant pigment anthocyanins, found in blueberries, black grapes and black raspberries to name just a few. Research proves this carotenoid is a powerful antioxidant helping to prevent certain types of cancer. It similarly plays a role in preventing diseases such as diabetes, dementia, stroke and heart disease.

This group furthermore contains vitamin C, fibre, lutein, zeaxanthin and other antioxidants, ellagic acid and flavonoids. Flavonoids are mainly found in dark grapes, blueberries and red berries although also present in garlic and onions. Both flavonoids and ellagic acid are also believed to have anti-cancer properties.

White

Garlic, white potatoes and onions are just a few members of the white group to provide exceptional health benefits for your little one. Garlic includes the compound 'allicin', the main reason for its many health promoting properties; believed to be anti-cancer, prevent heart disease, and reduce cholesterol and blood pressure. Garlic also possesses antibiotic

and anti-viral properties helping to protect against cold and flu viruses. In fact, garlic has so many health benefits entire books have been dedicated to this smelly (and yet very flavoursome) little herb, and due to its unique flavour is widely used in Indian cookery.

Root ginger, another potent herb from the white group is also used frequently in Indian cookery. Great for aiding digestion, treating fever from coughs and colds and is useful for treating arthritis.

White potatoes (in addition to being a starchy food), are an excellent source of potassium. Potassium is not only vital to heart function, it is a mineral essential for the entire body ensuring all cells, tissues and internal organs are kept in excellent working order. Another major source of potassium from the white group is bananas.

As well as containing flavonoids, onions are high in vitamin C, they are anti-cancer, and anti-inflammatory helping to protect the body against infections and allergies. Onions are heavily used in Indian cookery and form the base of most curry sauces.

So we've reached the end of the rainbow and you can see there are unquestionable benefits to eating a range of different coloured fruit and vegetables; all providing your little one with unique vitamins and minerals essential for a well-balanced diet.

Milk and Dairy Foods

Going back to our main food groups, this group includes all full-fat dairy produce - whole milk, cheese, yogurt, fromage frais and custard. All great sources of vitamin A and calcium, key to building strong teeth and bones. With the exception of whole milk, all are safe to introduce into your little ones diet from 6 months.

Whole milk MUST NOT be introduced into baby's diet as a main drink prior to the age of one, as it lacks the right balance of nutrients, vitamins and minerals. Continue with either breast or formula milk until your little ones first birthday. Whole milk can, however, be used in cooking prior to the age of one.

Feed your little one, three servings per day of her usual milk to ensure she has the correct amount of calcium required for healthy growth.

Milk and Dairy SuperFood: Yogurt

Yogurt was awarded its SuperFood status due to its probiotic properties which provide healthy bacteria for the gut. Gut health and good digestion are both linked to the overall health of the immune system. So it is imperative both are kept in good working order to give your little one the opportunity to fight off viruses and infections naturally.

Yogurt is furthermore high in iodine, necessary for healthy thyroid gland function. The thyroid gland supplies hormones to the body to control growth and metabolism, vital for weight control. It is similarly rich in calcium, protein and is easily digestible.

Protein-Rich

This group includes: lean red meat, poultry, fish, eggs, nuts and pulses (e.g. beans, lentils and peas); and foods made from pulses (e.g. tofu, hummus and soya foods).

Protein is essential for healthy growth because it lives in every cell and tissue in our body i.e. hair, muscle, skin, nails. Proteins are composed of different combinations of twenty amino acids broken down into 'essential' and 'non-essential' amino acids. Eight 'essential' amino acids must be consumed through food as our bodies cannot produce them naturally. The other twelve 'non-essential' amino acids can be produced daily by our bodies.

The protein-rich food group therefore provides fundamental sources of eight 'essential' amino acids required by adults, and a further seven required by children to sustain and repair muscles, blood vessels, bones and internal organs. The group also supplies the essential mineral iron, required for producing red blood cells to carry oxygen around the body. A lack of iron can lead to anaemia later in life.

Meat and fish are excellent sources of B vitamins and supply another essential mineral, zinc; required for good sense of taste and smell and for healing cuts and wounds quickly and effectively. Exactly what your little one will need when she starts running around, causing mischief!

Feed your little one, one or two servings from this group every day.

Protein-Rich SuperFood: Oily Fish

Oily Fish are SuperFoods not only due to their high-quality protein and zinc content, but they also contain essential omega 3 fatty acids. Omega 3 fatty acids must be consumed through food, found in tuna, salmon and mackerel amongst other seafood; required for good brain function, growth and development, and for keeping the heart healthy. They are also believed to be anti-inflammatory and anti-cancer.

Fats, Salt, Sugar, Oils

A fifth group exists that babies should not be exposed to, comprised of sugary foods or foods high in saturated fats. Fats are essential for providing concentrated energy in children under the age of two, provided they are unsaturated, healthy fats (good fats), such as whole milk, yogurt, cheese, oily fish and lean cuts of meat. Saturated fats (bad fats) such as burgers, fried chips or sugary cakes and biscuits should be avoided.

Salt should be avoided as it can damage a baby's kidneys due to their immature digestive system. In the first 6 months babies need less than 1g of salt per day which they usually get from breast or formula milk. Between 7 to 12 months this increases to 1g per day.

Equally, sugar must be avoided as it can damage a baby's growing teeth. Sometimes before their teeth have even emerged! It also gives babies excess energy leading to a higher risk of growing into obese and overweight children, leading to health problems later in life. Babies get their sugar from natural sources such as fruits, vegetables and their usual milk.

SuperFood: Olive Oil

Olive oil, although should be used sparingly when preparing your little ones meals, is a SuperFood. Research has shown the monounsaturated fat found in olive oil is good for the heart. Likewise, it is rich in antioxidants and contains the naturally occurring property 'oleocanthal', which is anti-inflammatory. With this in mind olive oil is used in the majority of my recipes. Other oils you can use include soya and rapeseed oil (aka vegetable oil). Alternatively you can cook with ghee (clarified butter) commonly used within Indian cookery.

Food Groups - Getting the Balance Right for Toddler

Estimated Average Requirements (EAR) for Energy:

1 - 3 years: boys 1,230kcal per day

girls 1,165 kcal per day

(Source: Department of Health, Dietary Reference values for Food Energy and Nutrients for the UK)

From the age of one, your little ones diet should consist of three balanced meals and two healthy snacks per day to achieve her required calorie intake.

When your little one reaches the budding age of two she will still need to consume three meals and two snacks per day, although her serving requirement from each food group will change. Up to the age of five her diet will take a gradual

shift towards that of an adult. So, from the age of two the UK 'eatwell plate' can be applied to her diet.

The eatwell plate is a handy visual guide to assist you in understanding how much of what your little one eats comes from each food group, including all of her snack requirements. An extensively tested model by the Department of Health, it represents how different foods contribute towards the overall balance of a healthy diet for an adult or child. An excellent tool you can refer to for the whole family.

Depending on what mood your little one is in, she may binge on food one day and barely eat anything the next. So use the eatwell plate as a guide to achieve a healthy balanced diet over a period of time i.e. a week rather than a day; and continue offering nutrient-rich foods and new tastes and textures where you can, to keep food interesting.

The eatwell plate

Use the eatwell plate to help you get the balance right.
It shows how much of what you eat should come from each food group.

Fruit and vegetables

Bread, rice, potatoes, pasta and other starchy foods

Meat, fish, eggs, beans and other non-dairy sources of protein

Foods and drinks high in fat and/or sugar

Milk and dairy foods

Welsh Government in association with Department of Health, the Scottish Government and the Food Standards Agency in Northern Ireland

Bread, Rice, Potatoes, Pasta and other Starchy foods

The food group I refer to as 'Carb-Rich (Starches)'.

Eat plenty. At least one third of your little ones food intake should be starchy foods. Continue feeding her a combination of white and wholemeal varieties to ensure she gets the correct amount of calories required for healthy growth and slow release energy.

Fruit and Vegetables

Fruit and vegetables make up another third of your little ones food requirements. So eat plenty and increase her servings gradually from three to four per day, to at least five servings per day. One serving equates to the amount your little one can hold in her hand.

As she grows, continue feeding her a rainbow of as many different coloured fruit and vegetables in each meal as you can to maintain her balanced diet.

Milk and Dairy Foods

Dairy is no longer a huge part of your little ones diet, but she will need to eat some. Between the ages of two and three years, continue offering her three servings of calcium per day. This can be achieved through 300ml (half a pint) of milk offered throughout the day with meals. Or by serving one glass of milk, and later offering some other dairy foods. Also, from the age of two, provided she is not underweight and is growing well, you can move your little one onto semi-skimmed milk if you wish.

As your little one approaches five, choose lower fat alternatives where possible to avoid unnecessary weight gain, or offer higher fat versions infrequently or in smaller amounts.

Meat, Fish, Eggs, Beans and other Non-Dairy Sources of Protein

The food group I refer to as 'Protein-Rich'.

Eat some. Continue to cook with lean servings of meat where possible as these contain lower amounts of fat. Alternatively, eat higher fat versions infrequently or in smaller amounts.

Feed your little one at least two servings of fish per week, including one serving of oily fish.

Foods and Drinks High in Fat and/or Sugar

Eat just a small amount. By this stage your little one will no doubt have been introduced to a few sweet treats either by yourself or by members of the family. Try to keep these to a minimum served only after a main meal to avoid tooth decay and unnecessary weight gain. Alternatively you can offer my Sweet SuperMeals as a healthy means to satisfy your little ones sweet tooth. Likewise, salt should be kept to a minimum. See guideline below.

Age	Maximum Salt Intake
1-3 years	2g per day
4-6 years	3g per day
7-10 years	5g per day
11 years - adults	6g per day

Foods to Avoid & Potential Allergens	Reason	Safe to Introduce at:
Drinks (caffeine and no-added sugar)i.e. tea, coffee, diet, no-added sugar squashes.	Fills baby's tummy unnecessarily. Tea and coffee reduces iron absorption.	Not required. Offer sips of water with meals.
Drinks (sweet) i.e. squash, fizzy drinks, fruit juices.	Contains a lot of added sugar which can lead to tooth decay and weight gain.	Not required. Offer sips of water with meals.
Eggs	Undercooked eggs may contain salmonella bacteria which can cause food poisoning. Eggs are also an allergen in infants under 12 months.	6 months + Provided the whole egg (yolk and white) are cooked thoroughly.
Fish bones	Choking hazard.	6 months + Fish is safe from 6 months provided all bones have been removed.
Fruits (Citrus) i.e. oranges, lemons, clementines, grapefruits.	Acidity can cause tummy upset and rashes (including nappy rash). Occasionally causes allergic reactions.	6 months + Introduce using the 'four day rule'.
Fruits (Other) Strawberries, raspberries, kiwi fruit.	Occasionally causes allergic reactions.	6 months + Introduce using the 'four day rule'.
Hard foods i.e. apple chunks, raw carrot sticks.	Choking hazard.	6 months + Lightly steam to soften.
Honey	Occasionally contains bacteria causing Infant botulism (serious illness of the intestines). Also a sugar so can cause tooth decay.	1 year +
Low-fat foods i.e. milk, yogurt, cheese etc.	Fat is an important source of concentrated energy for babies and toddlers, so full-fat varieties are essential for a minimum of 2 years.	2 years +
Raw shellfish	Can cause food poisoning.	Not required.
Shark, Swordfish, Marlin	Contain high levels of mercury which can affect a baby's developing nervous system.	Not required. Offer oily fish instead i.e. tuna, salmon, mackerel.
Small, round foods i.e. grapes, cherry tomatoes.	Choking hazard.	6 months + Cut into small pieces.
Sweet foods i.e. Indian sweets (mithai), chocolate, sweets.	Contain a lot of added sugar and saturated fat.	Not required.
Whole nuts (including peanuts).	Choking hazard. However can be crushed, ground or given to babies in the form of peanut butter after 6 months of age, providing they are not allergic.	5 years +

Getting Started - The Essentials

To get started you'll need to invest in some essentials for the kitchen. The most important being... spices! Spices can be very confusing if you haven't used them before, all with their own unique colours, flavours and aromas. Where do you start? Well, to take the confusion away, I have compiled two essential **'Spice Starter Kits'**.

'Spice Starter Kit 1' includes all of the core aromatic spices I use in my Stage 2 recipes. 'Spice Starter Kit 2' includes additional aromatic spices you will need to use alongside 'Spice Starter Kit 1', for Stage 3 and 4 recipes. I would recommend investing in 'Spice Starter Kit 1' first, and as your little one progresses into toddlerhood, investing in 'Spice Starter Kit 2'.

Spice Starter Kit 1 (Stage 2)

Black Pepper (ground)
Cardamom pods (green - ground or whole)
Cinnamon (ground)
Coriander (ground)
Cumin (ground)
Garlic (fresh or ready minced)
Ginger (fresh or ready minced)
Turmeric (ground)

Spice Starter Kit 2 (Stage 3 & 4)

Black Peppercorns (whole)
Cardamom pods (black, whole)
Cinnamon sticks (whole)
Cloves (whole)
Cumin seeds (whole)
Garam masala (ground)
Mild Paprika (ground)

Additional aromatic spices are used within Stages 2, 3 and 4 recipes such as saffron, nutmeg, mint and oregano amongst others. However, these spices are used infrequently so they can be bought when necessary.

Spice Advice

Spices are available in whole and ground varieties. If you prefer, you can buy spices whole and use a pestle and mortar to grind them into a powder. For convenience however, I kept both whole and ground spices in the cupboard.

IMPORTANT: ensure all spices you buy are produced by reputable brands, sealed with a clear expiry date on the packet. If you are unfamiliar with spice brands, I would recommend buying them from well-known supermarkets only. Once the packet is opened store in a clean, dry, air tight container away from sunlight to ensure the spices remain fresh for baby.

Other Essential Equipment:

- Baby/ toddler bowls
- Baby/ toddler spoons
- Bibs and/ or long-sleeved bibs
- Food processer/ handheld blender
- High-chair (with tray)
- Large-based non-stick frying pan
- Masher
- Medium and large sized pots (with lids)
- Olive oil
- Onions
- Pestle and mortar (optional)
- Steamer (optional)
- Unsalted butter
- Wooden spoon

Worth Knowing

- If your weekly shopping budget allows, buy organic produce for baby as the produce is free from artificial fertilisers and ensures a GM (genetically modified) free diet. Almost everything nowadays has an organic counterpart: milk, meat, vegetables, butter, cheese and yogurt. All are readily available from supermarkets.

- If you warm your little ones food in the microwave, please stir the food thoroughly to ensure there are no hot spots. You must ALWAYS test the temperature of your baby's food before serving.

- Curries taste their finest when you let them stand for about half an hour to an hour before serving, giving the spices a chance to soak into the meat, fish or vegetables. Even if the curries are refrigerated or frozen, the longer they stand, the better they taste!

- If you want to feed your little one curry with roti and she insists on feeding herself, break the roti into small pieces, top with curry and mix it altogether. She will happily eat the curry soaked pieces of roti (and any meat or vegetables) with her fingers, transforming the curry into a handy finger food.

Right then, we've gone through everything you'll need to know in order to cook your own SuperMeals, so let's get cooking!

Veggie SuperMeals

The Stage 2 recipes in this chapter are the scrumptious vegetarian SuperMeals I fed Aaliyah when she moved on from Stage 1 pureed fruit and veggies. I mashed the vegetables within these meals to achieve those much-needed **soft lumps** to help her learn to chew.

Chewing, an essential **motor skill** for baby gives the jaw, lips and tongue muscles an excellent work out. A crucial skill to master because the muscles used for chewing are the same muscles required to help baby **develop speech** later in childhood.

Don't worry if your baby is still a 'gummy baby' (doesn't have any teeth) at this stage, her hard little gums will be able to power through soft lumps easily enough.

You can offer meat and poultry to babies from 7 months of age in cooked, pureed form only, as meat proteins are not as easy to digest as vegetables. For this reason, I chose to wait until Aaliyah's digestive system had matured before introducing meat into her diet. In the meantime, I fed Aaliyah fish, eggs and lentils to ensure there were no protein shortfalls in her diet.

Please note **milk feeds** are still a huge part of baby's diet. She will need 500-600ml (1 pint) per day to ensure she receives the necessary amount of calcium required for healthy growth. So continue feeding your little one either breast or formula milk.

Sweet Potato, Apple and Dhal Curry

• •

Dhal (lentils) are a staple in many Indian and Pakistani households and are highly recommended for those following a strict vegetarian diet. The lentils provide a valuable source of protein that babies need for healthy growth, ensuring 'vegetarian babies' do not miss important nutrients from the protein-rich food group.

1 tbsp olive oil

1 small onion - peeled, finely chopped

¼ tsp minced ginger

¼ tsp minced garlic

Pinch of ground cumin

¼ tsp ground cinnamon

125g (4oz) red lentils - soaked in water (10mins), washed, drained

1 small sweet potato - washed, peeled, cubed

550ml (1 pint) of water

1 sweet apple - peeled, cored, chopped into small chunks

Heat the oil in a pot, add the onion and stir-fry for 3-4mins. Turn to low heat and add the ginger, garlic, cumin and cinnamon and stir-fry for a further 30secs.

Add the lentils to the pot, along with the sweet potato, cover with the water and stir. Bring to the boil and simmer (uncovered) on medium heat for 20mins, until both the lentils and potato are tender.

Whilst the lentils and potato are cooking, steam the apple chunks using a steamer or in the microwave by placing them in a microwavable dish and adding 2 tablespoons of water. Cover the dish with either a lid (leaving a small vent) or cling film (piercing a few holes), and steam on high for 1½-2mins until tender.

Once cooked, drain the excess water and add to the curry at the end. Stir and mash the whole curry to a consistency your little one will be comfortable eating. Delicious served on its own or with rice or roti for toddlers.

Ratatouille

• •

Inspired by the French classic this SuperMeal is chock-full with a range of vitamins, minerals, antioxidant and anti-cancer properties from a combination of the red, purple, green and white vegetables within this meal. Tomatoes, onions and courgettes (zucchinis) are all excellent sources of vitamin C contributing towards a healthy immune system. Courgettes are too rich in potassium, wonderful for heart health and for helping the body to absorb calcium for strong teeth and bones.

1 tbsp olive oil

1 onion - peeled, chopped

½ tsp minced garlic

2 baby aubergines/ eggplants - washed, peeled, finely diced

1 small courgette/ zucchini - washed, finely diced

½ red bell pepper - washed, deseeded, finely diced

200g (7oz) tinned chopped tomatoes

¼ tsp dried oregano

Pinch of ground black pepper

75ml (3fl oz) of water

30g (1¼oz) medium Cheddar cheese - grated (optional)

Heat the oil in a large frying pan, add the onion and stir-fry on medium-low heat for 2-3mins. Add the garlic, aubergines, courgette, red bell pepper and stir-fry for 10mins.

Add the tomatoes, oregano, black pepper, water and stir. Simmer (covered) on medium-low heat for another 10mins. Check halfway, if the sauce looks dry add some extra water, replace the lid and continue to cook.

When all of the vegetables are tender, turn off the heat, sprinkle over the cheese (if using) and fold in until melted. Blend if necessary to achieve the required lumpy consistency using a pulse motion. Serve on its own or with cooked pasta.

Kitchri

• •

'Kitchri' (yellow lentil rice) is traditionally eaten with 'Kadhi' (yogurt soup). I however, chose to serve it alongside most curries I fed Aaliyah because Kitchri is 'SuperRice' in my opinion. Here's why: the rice provides complex carbohydrates for energy, the lentils add protein, turmeric adds a powerful cold and flu preventing ingredient, and cardamom adds a natural painkiller for teething. I rest my case!

1 tbsp yellow lentils (toor dhal) - soaked in water (10mins), washed, drained

100g (3½oz) brown basmati rice - soaked in water (10mins), washed, drained

Pinch of ground turmeric

Pinch of ground cardamom - green

1 tbsp vegetable oil

550ml (1 pint) of water

Add the lentils, rice, turmeric, cardamom, oil and water to the pot and stir. Bring to the boil and simmer (covered) on low heat for 40-45mins, until the lentils and rice are both tender and all of the water has been absorbed. The rice should be overcooked to a mushy consistency which will make it easier for baby to chew and swallow.

Serve warm as an accompaniment to curry or as a yummy snack by adding my Bananaberry Raita (page 101) to the kitchri.

Mint and Coriander Veggie Stew

• •

Hearty and delicious! Not only is this a well-balanced meal utilising almost every food group, the antioxidant spice mint adds extra health benefits by aiding digestion and protecting against unsettled tummies. Mint is also great for opening congested nasal and throat passages, so I would recommend this comforting SuperMeal if your little one has the cold or flu.

Heat the oil in a pot, add the onion and stir-fry for 3-4mins. Turn to low heat and add the ginger, garlic, coriander and turmeric. Continue to stir-fry for 30secs-1min until the aroma from the spices has been released.

Add the red and yellow lentils to the pot along with the potato, carrot, tomatoes and stir to coat the vegetables in the delicious spices. Pour the water into the pot and add the bay leaf and mint. Bring to the boil and simmer (covered) on low heat until tender.

Once tender, gently break the vegetables into soft lumps using the back of your wooden spoon. Remove the bay leaf and serve warm. Delicious served on its own, or for a heavier meal serve with soft buttered bread.

1 tbsp olive oil

1 onion - peeled, chopped

¼ tsp minced ginger

¼ tsp minced garlic

Pinch of ground coriander

Pinch of ground turmeric

1 tbsp red lentils - soaked in water (10mins), washed, drained

1 tbsp yellow lentils (toor dhal) - soaked in water (10mins), washed, drained

1 small white potato - washed, peeled, cubed

1 medium carrot - washed, peeled, finely chopped

80g (3oz) cherry tomatoes - washed, deseeded, chopped

550ml (1 pint) of water

1 bay leaf

Pinch of dried mint

Mixed Veggies in Coconut Milk

UK healthcare professionals actively campaign 'breast is best' for newborn babies due to the perfect nutritional content of breast milk, and its immune-boosting compound 'lauric acid'. Only one other natural source exists close enough to match the lauric acid content found in breast milk, and it can be found in coconuts. Although coconut oil is by far the most concentrated source, it can be found in desiccated coconut and in coconut milk. So feeding your little one this creamy scrummy curry should help to keep infections at bay.

Heat the oil in a pot, add the onion and stir-fry on medium-low heat for 3-4mins until soft and golden. Turn to low heat and add garlic, ginger, turmeric, cumin, coriander and stir-fry for a further 30secs-1min.

Add all of the remaining vegetables to the pot along with the coconut milk and stir. Bring to the boil and simmer (covered) on a medium-low heat for 6-8mins until all of the vegetables are tender. Once cooked, mash the vegetables to a soft lumpy consistency using either a masher or blender using a pulse motion.

Serve to baby warm or for toddlers serve with rice or roti for a heavier meal.

1 tbsp olive oil

1 small onion - peeled, chopped

½ tsp minced garlic

¼ tsp minced ginger

Pinch of ground turmeric

Pinch of ground cumin

Pinch of ground coriander

1 medium parsnip - washed, peeled, chopped

70g (3oz) green beans - washed, ends chopped, halved

200g (7oz) cauliflower florets - washed, chopped (no stems)

100g (3½oz) tinned sweet corn (no added salt) - drained

250ml (8fl oz) unsweetened coconut milk

Veggie Korma

I love this recipe! It's simple, nutritious and includes the subtle and naturally sweet taste of the exotic coconut. Not widely accepted as a SuperFood just yet due to its fat content; coconuts are antioxidant, anti-viral, anti-bacterial, anti-fungal (great for nappy rash protection) and boost energy and immune system function. Equally coconuts are rich in fibre, vitamins and minerals. With all of these health benefits and more, coconuts are definitely SuperFoods in my opinion.

Heat the oil in a pot and add the tomato, turmeric, cumin, garlic and stir-fry for 1-2mins. Add the potato, coconut and water. Stir and bring to the boil. Simmer (covered) on low heat for 15-20mins until tender. Then mash and set aside.

Whilst the potato is boiling, steam the carrot and peas in either a steamer or in the microwave by placing them in a microwavable dish and adding 2 tablespoons of water. Cover the dish with either a lid (leaving a small vent) or cling film (piercing a few holes), and steam on high for 1-1½mins. Drain and add to the mashed potato. Further mash or blend as necessary using a pulse motion. Serve to baby warm.

1 tbsp olive oil

1 tomato - washed, deseeded, grated

Pinch of ground turmeric

Pinch of ground cumin

¼ tsp minced garlic

1 medium white potato - washed, peeled, cubed

2 tbsp unsweetened desiccated coconut

200ml (7fl oz) of water

1 medium carrot - peeled, washed, chopped

40g (1½oz) peas - frozen, washed

Rainbow Veggie Pie

This scrumptious pie epitomizes the concept of 'feeding your little one a rainbow'. Packed with red, green, orange and white vegetables, this pie is loaded with a range of vitamins and minerals perfectly balanced for your little one. Also including starchy foods and dairy, this pie utilises almost every food group.

1 tbsp olive oil

1 small onion - peeled, chopped

½ tsp minced garlic

1 tomato - washed, deseeded, chopped

Pinch of ground cumin

Pinch of ground coriander

1 medium carrot - peeled, washed, chopped

1 small sweet potato - washed, peeled, cubed

1 medium white potato - washed, peeled, cubed

400ml (14fl oz) of water

80g (3oz) broccoli florets - washed, chopped (no stems)

60g (2½oz) peas - frozen, washed

40g (1½oz) medium Cheddar cheese - grated

1-2 tbsp of whole milk (optional)

Heat the oil in a large pot, add the onion and stir-fry on medium-low heat for 3-4mins until soft and lightly golden. Turn to low heat and add the garlic, tomato, cumin and coriander and stir-fry for 2mins.

Add the carrot, sweet potato and white potato, pour in the water and stir. Bring to the boil and simmer (covered) on medium-low heat for 15mins. Add the broccoli and peas and continue to simmer for a further 5-7mins or until all of the vegetables are tender.

Sprinkle the cheese over the cooked vegetables in the pot, fold in until melted and mash to achieve a soft lumpy consistency. Add some milk to make it smoother if necessary. Serve to baby warm.

Warming Carrot and Broccoli Soup

I created this soup when Aaliyah suffered from her first cold. It includes valuable cold and flu fighting ingredients. The broccoli and bell pepper provide the vitamin C, the garlic's anti-viral properties provide cold and flu protection, and the ginger is excellent for treating fever and coughs. Combined with powerful SuperSpices, this soup will chase that pesky cold away in no time.

Heat the oil in a pot and add the onion, cardamom, clove and stir-fry on medium-low heat for 2-3mins. Then add the ginger, garlic and stir-fry on low heat for a further 30secs-1min.

Add the remaining vegetables to the pot followed by the turmeric, black pepper, cumin and stir. Pour the water into the pot, bring to the boil and simmer (covered) on a medium-low heat for 6-8mins until all of the vegetables are tender. Allow cooling and blend until smooth. Serve to baby warm on its own or with soft brown bread.

IMPORTANT: remove cardamom pod and clove before serving to baby.

1 tbsp olive oil

1 onion - peeled, chopped

1 whole cardamom pod - green

1 whole clove

½ tsp minced ginger

½ tsp minced garlic

2 medium carrots - peeled, washed, diced

200g (7oz) broccoli - washed, chopped (no stems)

1 red bell pepper - washed, deseeded, chopped

Pinch of ground turmeric

Pinch of ground black pepper

¼ tsp ground cumin

300ml (½ pint) of water

Yummy Spiced Potato Pie

• •

This Indian influenced potato pie is lightly flavoured with lots of traditional fragrant spices, which complement the white and sweet potato beautifully. Bursting with beta-carotene goodness this pie is great for healthy eyes and skin. The peas too provide antioxidant and anti-inflammatory properties making this fluffy, scrummy pie wonderfully nutritious.

1 medium white potato - washed, peeled, cubed

1 medium sweet potato - washed, peeled, cubed

1 tbsp olive oil

1 onion - peeled, finely chopped

¼ tsp minced garlic

Pinch of ground turmeric

Pinch of ground cumin

Pinch of ground coriander

Pinch of ground black pepper

60g (2½oz) peas - frozen, washed

1 tsp unsalted butter

2 tbsp of whole milk

Place the white and sweet potatoes in a pot and cover with cold water. Bring to the boil and simmer (uncovered) on medium-high heat for 10-12mins until tender.

Whilst the potatoes are boiling, heat the oil in a frying pan and add the onion. Stir-fry on medium-low heat until soft and golden. Add the garlic, turmeric, cumin, coriander, black pepper and stir-fry continuously for 30secs-1min to lightly cook the spices and set aside.

Next steam the peas in a steamer or in the microwave by placing them in a microwavable dish and adding 2 tablespoons of water. Cover the dish with either a lid (leaving a small vent) or cling film (piercing a few holes), and steam on high for 1-1½mins. Drain and set aside.

Once the potatoes are cooked, drain, place in a bowl and add the peas, butter, milk and mash the potatoes until smooth. Add the spiced onion and combine for a creamy, tasty pie. If the consistency is too heavy, add some extra milk. Serve to baby warm.

Festive Roasted Vegetable Mash

A great one for the festive period this meal is loaded with traditional Christmas flavours for baby – apples, rosemary, carrots and parsnips with a hint of Indian spices. Roasting vegetables are a fabulous way to maintain flavour and nutrients, so rest assured your little one will reap the health benefits of this meal. The vitamin A (in the form of beta-carotene) from the carrots, and the SuperSpice cumin, both help to support the development of a strong and healthy immune system.

½ tbsp olive oil

¼ tsp minced garlic

Pinch of ground black pepper

Pinch of ground cumin

1 medium carrot – peeled, washed, sliced (diagonally) into 1cm pieces

1 medium parsnip – peeled, washed, sliced (diagonally) into 1cm pieces

1 sprig of rosemary

Pure unsweetened apple juice

Pre-heat the oven to 220C/ 425F/ gas mark 7.

Add olive oil, garlic, black pepper and cumin into a bowl and stir. Then add the vegetables to the bowl and coat with the seasoning.

Lay the vegetables flat on top of a foil-covered baking tray and add 2 small branches of rosemary (broken off the sprig), on either side of the tray for a light flavour whilst roasting. Place the baking tray on the middle shelf of the oven and roast for 20-25mins until tender ensuring to turn over the vegetables half way.

Once tender, remove from the oven and take out the rosemary branches. Mash or puree as necessary and use as much apple juice as required to loosen the mash. Serve to baby warm.

Alternatively offer the roasted vegetables to your little one as a selection of finger foods when she is ready.

Note: the amount of time the vegetables take to roast depends on their thickness i.e. chunkier vegetables will take longer, equally thin cut vegetables will be quicker.

Butternut Squash, Apricot & Dhal Curry

• •

Also known as the 'Super Orange' curry as it is loaded with beta-carotene; great for healthy eyes, skin and immune system. One for the toddlers this one goes up a level in the spice and taste stakes. A healthy yet unusual curry combination that I guarantee your little one will enjoy.

2 tbsp olive oil

1 onion - peeled, chopped

1 tsp minced garlic

1 tsp minced ginger

200g (7oz) tinned chopped tomatoes

½ tsp ground garam masala

¼ tsp ground cumin

¼ tsp ground coriander

90g (3½oz) red lentils - soaked in water (10mins), washed, drained

½ butternut squash - peeled, cut into 1" chunks

60g (2½oz) dried apricots - finely chopped

1 tbsp unsweetened desiccated coconut

550ml (1 pint) of water

Heat the oil in a pot, add the onion and stir-fry on medium-low heat for 5mins until golden brown. Add the garlic, ginger and stir-fry for 30secs-1min then add the tomatoes, garam masala, cumin, coriander and stir-fry for a further 2mins to lightly cook the spices.

Finally add the lentils, squash, apricots, coconut, water and stir. Bring to the boil and simmer (covered) on medium-low heat for 20-25mins until the lentils are cooked and the squash is tender and breaks apart easily. Serve with quinoa, roti or rice.

Indian Vegetable Paella

A fragrant delicious paella packed with chunky vegetables, a firm favourite with Aaliyah. The bright sun-yellow rice acquires its colour from the SuperSpice turmeric, used as a natural colouring agent for generations. Turmeric, in addition to being a cold and flu prevention remedy is a source of iron and manganese. Iron is vital for transporting oxygen around the body, and the antioxidant mineral manganese is necessary for normal brain and nervous system function.

Place the rice in a pot, pour over the stock and add the turmeric, vegetable oil, saffron and stir. Bring to the boil and simmer (covered) on low heat for 10mins or until tender.

Whilst the rice is cooking, heat the olive oil in a frying pan and toss in the red bell pepper, courgette, garlic, black pepper and dried mixed herbs. Stir-fry for 6-7mins until tender.

Once the rice is cooked, add to the frying pan and combine with the vegetables. Mash or blend if necessary and serve to baby warm.

100g (3½oz) white basmati rice - washed, drained

350ml (12fl oz) hot vegetable stock - baby friendly

¼ tsp ground turmeric

½ tbsp vegetable oil

3 saffron strands

½ tbsp olive oil

50g (2oz) red bell pepper - washed, deseeded, finely diced

50g (2oz) courgette/ zucchini - washed, finely diced

1 tsp minced garlic

Pinch of ground black pepper

¼ tsp dried mixed herbs

Quick Cumin Spaghetti

Being so quick and simple to prepare, my preference was to make this meal fresh every time. Cooked using whole cumin seeds, these SuperSpices are tiny, yet offer a unique peppery taste which adds lots of flavour to this meal. Equally they are iron-rich, excellent for digestion and for boosting baby's immune system to help keep all of those horrible viruses at bay.

20g (¾ oz) spaghetti - broken into small pieces

40g (1½oz) broccoli florets - washed, chopped (no stems)

40g (1½oz) carrots - peeled, washed, diced

1 tbsp olive oil

¼ tsp cumin seeds

½ tsp minced garlic

Pinch of ground black pepper

¼ tsp dried mixed herbs

Cook the spaghetti pieces according to packet instructions.

Steam the broccoli and carrots in a steamer or in a microwave by placing them in a microwavable dish and adding 2 tablespoons of water. Cover the dish with either a lid (leaving a small vent) or cling film (piercing a few holes), and steam on high for 1-1½mins until tender. Once cooked, drain the excess water and set aside.

Heat the oil in a frying pan on low heat and add the cumin seeds, garlic, black pepper and herbs. Stir-fry for 2-3mins to lightly cook the spices. Then add the steamed vegetables and stir-fry altogether for another minute.

Drain the cooked spaghetti, toss into the frying pan with the vegetables and combine well. Serve to baby warm.

Quinoa Pilaf with Mixed Veggies

Quinoa, a grain bursting with protein goodness is an excellent food for strong growth and for keeping the whole body healthy. Highly recommended for 'vegetarian babies', this is a hassle-free, throw everything into one pot meal with lots of chunky vegetables; making this one suitable for a more experienced chewer.

1½ tbsp olive oil

1 onion - peeled, chopped

½ tsp minced ginger

1 tsp minced garlic

1 tomato - washed, diced

50g (2oz) cauliflower florets - washed, chopped (no stems)

40g (1½oz) peas -frozen, washed

1 medium carrot - peeled, washed, finely diced

Squeeze of ½ a lemon - ensuring no seeds fall in

½ tsp ground garam masala

½ tsp ground coriander

¼ tsp ground turmeric

80g (3oz) quinoa - soaked in water (10mins), washed, drained

300ml (½ pint) of water

Heat oil in the pot, add the onion and stir-fry on medium-low heat for 3mins until soft. Add the ginger, garlic and stir-fry for a further 30secs-1min, followed by the tomato, cauliflower, peas, carrots, lemon juice and spices (garam masala, coriander, and turmeric). Stir everything together so the vegetables are coated in the delicious spices and stir-fry for 2mins.

Finally add the quinoa to the pot along with the water and stir. Bring to the boil and simmer (covered) on low heat for 20-25mins until all of the vegetables are tender (checking halfway). Serve to baby warm with my mint yogurt raita (page 109).

Alternatively steam the cauliflower, peas and carrots separately in either a steamer or in the microwave by placing them in a microwavable dish and adding 2 tablespoons of water. Cover the dish with either a lid (leaving a small vent) or cling film (piercing a few holes), and steam on high for 1-2mins or until tender. Stir into the cooked quinoa and serve.

Fish SuperMeals

As mentioned, fish was a vital part of Aaliyah's diet from the age of 7 months because I chose not to feed her meat until she was 10 months old, making fish a fantastic meat protein substitute.

To begin with I introduced white fish into her diet as these are quite mild in taste - cod, coley and pollock amongst others. I then followed up with slightly stronger tasting oily fish - salmon and tuna.

I loved just how much Aaliyah enjoyed eating fish, not only due to their essential omega 3 fatty acid and essential amino acid content, but because fish is so quick and easy to cook! Being a mother and having a million things to do meant fish was perfect for cooking quick, wholesome meals.

I kept bags of freshly frozen white fish and salmon in the freezer. Whenever I decided today was 'fish day' or was short for time, I'd simply take one fillet out of the freezer, and poach it in the microwave. It was cooked and flaky within a matter of minutes.

A little reminder:

- Avoid fish containing high levels of mercury (shark, swordfish and marlin), as these can affect a baby's developing nervous system.

- Ensure all bones have been removed before serving.

Fish Pie with Pepper and Coriander

White fish, although doesn't contain the same SuperFood health benefits as oily fish, still has wonderful health benefits for your little one. Protein-rich and high in B vitamins suggests lots of energy after eating this meal. Combined with the black pepper and coriander to aid digestion, this is a perfect first fish dish for baby.

Place the potatoes in a pot and cover with cold water. Bring to the boil and simmer for 15mins until tender.

Whilst the potatoes are boiling, heat the oil in a frying pan, add the onion and stir-fry for 3-4mins until golden. Then add the garlic, all four spices and stir-fry for a further 30secs-1min, and set aside.

Place the fish in a microwavable dish, gently rub in the butter and spoon over half of the milk. Cover the dish with either a lid (leaving a small vent) or cling film (piercing a few holes), and poach in the microwave on high for 1½-2mins until the fish is flaky. Check half way to ensure the fish has not been overcooked.

Once the potatoes are cooked, drain and place in a bowl. Add the remaining milk (along with the buttery milk the fish was cooked in) and mash the potatoes until smooth. Add the spiced onion and flake the fish into the mash, ensuring there are no sneaky bones left. Combine together for a creamy, luscious pie. If the pie consistency is too heavy for baby, add some extra milk. Serve warm.

2 small white potatoes - peeled, washed, cubed

1 tbsp olive oil

1 onion - peeled, finely chopped

¼ tsp minced garlic

Pinch of ground turmeric

Pinch of ground cumin

Pinch of ground coriander

Pinch of ground black pepper

1 x 100g (3½oz) white fish fillet (skinless, boneless)

1 tsp unsalted butter - softened

4 tbsp of whole milk

Sweet Fish and Fruit Curry

• •

A creamy super quick fish curry with just the right amount of sweetness and spice to tickle little taste buds without overwhelming them. This curry is protein-rich and packed with fruity SuperFood goodness of the apple, pear and banana. These fruits are antioxidant and high in fibre, keeping little bowels healthy by preventing constipation.

1 sweet apple - peeled, cored, cubed

1 ripe pear - peeled, cored, cubed

1 banana - peeled, sliced

2 tbsp plain unsweetened yogurt

150ml (5fl oz) of whole milk

¼ tsp minced ginger

¼ tsp minced garlic

¼ tsp ground cumin

¼ tsp ground coriander

Pinch of ground black pepper

Pinch of ground turmeric

1 x 100g (3½oz) white fish fillet (skinless, boneless) - cut into 1" chunks

Place the fruit, yogurt, milk, ginger, garlic and spices (cumin, coriander, black pepper and turmeric), into a blender and blend until smooth. Pour the fruity mixture into a pot, bring to the boil and simmer (uncovered) on low heat for 5mins to ensure all the spices are cooked through, stirring occasionally.

Add the fish chunks to the sauce and continue to simmer for a further 5-6mins, until the fish is flaky and breaks apart easily. Serve with plain overcooked rice, kitchri (page 40) or roti (page 88).

IMPORTANT: ensure there are no fish bones included within baby's serving. You can do this by breaking the fish pieces with your fingers just before serving.

Creamy Tuna Loaded Potato Skins

• •

A great meal to coax your little one in to eating tuna, a hugely beneficial oily fish packed with essential omega 3 fatty acids, essential amino acids (protein) and B vitamins. A stronger tasting fish no doubt, but the sweet potato complements the strong flavour of the tuna beautifully making this an exceptionally scrummy meal.

Place the sweet potato in the microwave and cook on high for 6-7mins until tender to the touch. Once cooled (but still warm enough to melt the cream cheese), cut the potato in half lengthways, scoop out the flesh and place it in a bowl.

Flake in the tuna and add the cream cheese, black pepper, and mixed herbs. Combine and mash all of the ingredients together whilst ensuring some soft lumps have been left. Spoon the mixture back into the jackets if you wish, although it is not essential. Serve to baby warm.

1 medium sweet potato - scrubbed, washed, pricked all around

90g (3¼oz) tinned tuna (in spring water) - drained

1 tbsp full fat cream cheese

Pinch of ground black pepper

Pinch of dried mixed herbs (optional)

Desi Mac 'n' Cheese with Tuna

An Indian twist on a British school dinner classic... loaded with complex carbohydrates vital for energy (courtesy of the macaroni pasta), this meal is extremely versatile. Exclude the tuna for a vegetarian meal, chop up cooked macaroni for spoon-feeding, or keep the macaroni pasta whole and serve as a finger food.

Cook the macaroni according to packet instructions. Once cooked, drain and set aside.

Tomato masala: Heat the oil in a frying pan, add the onion and stir-fry on medium-low heat for 2mins until soft. Add the garlic, ginger, tomato, oregano and stir-fry continuously for a few minutes until the tomato chunks begin to soften, and set aside.

White sauce: In a pot, melt the butter on low heat and spoon in the flour. Stir continuously until a paste is formed, then pour in the milk a little at a time and whisk vigorously to avoid any lumps appearing. Once all of the milk has been poured, add the nutmeg, black pepper and flake in the tuna. Bring to the boil on low heat and simmer (uncovered) for 4-5mins, stirring occasionally. Once cooked, add the cheese and the tomato masala to the sauce and stir. If the sauce looks very heavy, add some extra milk.

Toss the cooked macaroni into sauce and combine well. Serve to baby warm.

80g (3oz) macaroni pasta

Tomato masala:
1 tbsp olive oil
½ onion- peeled, chopped
½ tsp minced garlic
½ tsp minced ginger
1 tomato - washed, chopped
¼ tsp dried oregano

White sauce:
2 tbsp unsalted butter
2 tbsp plain flour
350ml (12fl oz) of whole milk
Pinch of ground nutmeg
Pinch of ground black pepper
1 x 185g (6½oz) tinned tuna (in spring water) - drained
30g (1oz) medium Cheddar cheese - grated

Indian Salmon Risotto

Salmon contains all of the SuperFood health benefits of oily fish, and encompasses another major one, being rich in vitamin D - the 'Sunshine Vitamin'. Essential for building strong muscles and bones (by regulating calcium in the body), this vitamin is vital for helping your little one learn to walk. Although the best source of vitamin D is the sunshine, this mouth-watering textured risotto will add an extra little boost into her diet.

1 tbsp olive oil

1 small onion - peeled, chopped

¼ tsp minced ginger

½ tsp minced garlic

Pinch of ground nutmeg

Pinch of ground cumin

Pinch of ground black pepper

1 curry leaf

100g (3½ oz) Arborio risotto rice - washed, drained

750ml (1¼ pint) of hot vegetable or fish stock - baby-friendly

60g (2½oz) parsnip - peeled, washed, cubed

60g (2½oz) broccoli florets - washed, chopped (no stems)

1 x 100g (3½oz) salmon fillet (skinless, boneless)

1 tsp unsalted butter- softened

2 tbsp of whole milk

Heat the oil in a pot, add the onion and stir-fry for 4-5mins until golden. Then add the ginger, garlic, all of the spices and lightly cook for 30secs-1min. Add the rice and stock to the pot, stir and bring to the boil. Simmer (covered) on a low heat for 15-20mins until creamy and tender.

Whilst the rice is cooking, steam the parsnip and broccoli in a steamer or in the microwave by placing them in a microwavable dish and adding 2 tablespoons of water. Cover the dish with either a lid (leaving a small vent) or cling film (piercing a few holes), and steam on high for 1½-2mins until tender. Once cooked, drain and set aside.

Next place the salmon in a microwavable dish, gently rub in the butter and spoon over the milk. Poach in the microwave (covered leaving a small vent) for 2-3mins until the fish is flaky. Check half way to ensure the fish has not been overcooked.

Once the rice is cooked, add the steamed veggies and flake in the salmon ensuring there are no sneaky bones left. Combine together for a delicious, aromatic meal.

Finger Food SuperMeals

Finger foods are bite-sized or stick shaped pieces of food babies can pick up with their podgy little fingers to feed themselves with, known as **baby-led weaning** or self-feeding. Great for baby's hand to eye co-ordination and for her independence, so should be encouraged with lots of enthusiastic clapping and cheering from mummy and daddy.

The two other benefits of self-feeding include: **healthier eating habits**, as babies are naturally drawn towards carbohydrates, and weight control. As self-fed babies are in control of their own appetite, they are more likely to be a healthier weight over spoon-fed babies.

I chose to use both spoon-feeding and self-feeding techniques with Aaliyah. Spoon-feeding was adopted at main meal times whereas self-feeding was encouraged at snack times. I found this routine worked perfectly for us. For me because I knew Aaliyah had eaten well; for Aaliyah so she could practice using her pincer grip allowing her to perfect her motor skills.

'Gummy babies' can still eat finger foods. Just be certain the food you have prepared can be mushed easily between little gums and will melt-in-the-mouth.

If your little one is not **exploring food** with her hands or self-feeding at 7 months, she will at some point. So I would recommend investing in some long-sleeved bibs and plastic mats (or throw down a towel) for the floor as things are going to get very messy!

Please be vigilant when babies are self-feeding as finger foods are a choking hazard. Babies should be supervised at all times.

Appleberry French Toast

A delicious soft, fluffy, finger food made with a fruity blend of naturally sweet apple juice combined with the popular SuperFood blueberries. In addition to their well-known antioxidant power, blueberries are great for eye health, improving memory and providing a concentrated source of vitamin K.

40g (1½oz) blueberries - fresh, washed

1 egg yolk (optional)

100ml (3½fl oz) of whole milk

50ml (2fl oz) pure unsweetened apple juice

Sprinkle of ground cinnamon

2 slices of bread - white

2 knobs of unsalted butter

Add the blueberries, egg yolk, whole milk, apple juice and cinnamon into a blender and blend until smooth. Then pour the mixture into a dish large enough to dip a slice of bread in.

Place one slice of bread in the dish face down and let it soak for a few seconds without letting it get soggy. Turn it over and repeat on the other side.

Heat one knob of butter in a frying pan and gently place the slice of bread in. Cook on medium heat for a few minutes until golden brown and repeat on the other side. If you are using egg, you must ensure both sides are cooked thoroughly.

Once cooked, cut the french toast into strips or bite-size pieces and serve to baby warm. Repeat the process for the second slice of bread.

Tip: for an authentic French toast recipe, remove the blueberries and apple juice and replace them with a few drops of vanilla.

Minted Green Beans

Naturally grown in a handy finger food shape, green beans are bursting with nutrients. Containing antioxidant vitamins A and C, the antioxidant mineral manganese (required for strong bone structure) and vitamin K, necessary for blood clotting to heal cuts and wounds effectively.

Pour the stock into a pot, add the mint, nutmeg and bring to the boil.

Then add the green beans to the stock and simmer (uncovered) on a medium heat for 5-6mins until the beans are tender.

Once cooked, remove from the pot, drain, and serve to baby warm on its own, or with my mint yogurt raita (page 109) as a tasty dip.

Tip: if you are cooking with fresh green beans, test the freshness by 'snapping' them before you buy as the 'snap' is the sign of a healthy bean.

80g (3oz) green beans - washed, ends chopped, halved

250ml (8fl oz) hot vegetable stock - baby friendly

Pinch of dried mint

Pinch of ground nutmeg

Sweet Egg Curry

Serve as a delicious lunch or dinner, an excellent protein-rich meal chock-full of SuperSpice goodness, incorporating a range of health benefits from the spices including anti-bacterial protection (turmeric); preventative treatment against dry skin and eczema (coriander), and healthy digestion and bowels (from all of the spices).

Crack the egg into a bowl, spoon in the milk, add the black pepper and whisk. Then set aside.

Heat the oil in a frying pan, add the onion and stir-fry on low heat for 2mins until golden. Then add tomato, ginger, garlic, turmeric, coriander and cook for 2mins until the tomato is soft.

Pour the whisked egg to the frying pan and stir-fry on low heat until the egg is well-cooked and light and fluffy in texture. Pop the banana into the frying pan and stir-fry for a few seconds.

Allow cooling before serving to baby as a yummy, squidgy finger food. Or for older babies serve with roti for a more filling meal.

Tip: for a savoury taste simply omit the banana.

½ tbsp olive oil

½ onion - peeled, chopped

1 egg

1 tbsp of whole milk

Pinch of ground black pepper

½ tomato - washed, deseeded, finely chopped

¼ tsp minced ginger

¼ tsp minced garlic

Pinch of ground turmeric

Pinch of ground coriander

½ banana - peeled, cubed

Warm Buttery Pitta Bread

● ●

Popular in Middle-Eastern, Mediterranean and Indian cuisine, pitta bread is a quick, healthy snack to provide your little one with a wholegrain boost between meals. The complex carbohydrates in the pitta ensure energy is released slowly to keep her going until her next meal time.

1 wholemeal pitta bread - ready-made

Knob of unsalted butter or ghee

Place the pitta bread in the toaster for 2-3mins until warm, but not crispy. Alternatively warm it in the grill, oven or microwave.

Then lay the pitta on a plate and spread the butter or ghee over it. Cut into slices and serve to baby on its own.

For older babies serve with my aubergine bharta (dip) on page 93. Also delicious served with any of my curries as an alternative to roti.

Seasoned Sweet Potato Fries

If your little one is teething, this tasty snack may help to sooth those uncomfortable symptoms. The nutmeg not only provides a warm, aromatic taste to complement the sweet potato, it also contains the compound 'eugenol', which is used as a natural medicine to treat toothaches. Combined with the powerful analgesic properties of cinnamon, this is a wonderful snack to combat teething pains.

½ tbsp olive oil

¼ tsp ground cinnamon

Pinch of ground nutmeg

1 small sweet potato - peeled, washed, cut into 2" sticks

Pre-heat the oven to 200C/400F/gas mark 6.

In a bowl add the oil, cinnamon, nutmeg and stir. Add the potato sticks and give them a good toss to coat with the seasoning. Lay them flat on a foil-covered baking tray and place on the middle shelf.

Bake for 20-25mins or until tender, turning over half way. Allow cooling before serving to baby.

Roti sticks

• •

Yummy! Freshly made home-cooked roti's (chapattis) are delicious, soft and melt-in-the-mouth. Aaliyah loved eating them either on their own, or smeared with a little unsalted butter and a tiny sprinkling of ground cinnamon. Roti is a wonderful healthy snack for baby. Being a starchy food it provides your little one with lots of energy for playing and moving around.

150g (5oz) wholemeal chapatti/ atta flour

1 tbsp vegetable oil

250ml (8fl oz) of hot water

Place the flour and oil in a bowl and add water a little at a time and stir. Continue adding water until a soft (but not sticky) dough ball is formed. Then remove the dough ball from the bowl and knead for 1-2mins.

Divide the dough into 8 pieces and shape into small round balls. Sprinkle some flour over the counter and rolling pin so the dough doesn't stick and roll one of the balls until it resembles a flat, round 10" pancake. Repeat this process for all dough balls.

Heat a large frying pan or thava (round, flat frying pan), and cook one roti on medium heat until bubbles appear on the surface and the roti begins to brown. Turn it over and cook until bubbles appear on the other side. Then flip the roti at regular intervals until begins to puff up. Remove and set aside. Repeat for all roti's.

Once cooked, spread a little unsalted butter over the fresh roti, cut into strips and serve immediately whilst still warm. Alternatively you can freeze them for later. See page 188 for storage details.

Scrambled Egg with Cheese and Onion

An excellent high-quality protein ensuring your little one receives at least one of her 'two a day' portion from the protein-rich food group. Served as delicious breakfast, this will be a great start to her day.

Heat the oil in a frying pan, add the onion and stir-fry on medium-low heat for 2mins until golden. Whilst the onion is cooking, crack the egg into a bowl, add the milk, black pepper and whisk.

Once the onion is cooked, turn to low heat and add the egg mixture to the pan. Gently stir-fry the egg until it is cooked to a soft, fluffy texture. Switch off the stove and sprinkle over the cheese. Fold it in until it melts and is combined well with the egg.

Serve to baby as a tasty, squidgy finger food. For older babies serve with roti or buttered wholemeal toast as a delicious breakfast.

1 tbsp olive oil

½ onion - peeled, chopped

1 egg

1 tbsp of whole milk

Pinch of ground black pepper

7g (¼ oz) medium Cheddar cheese - grated

Aubergine Bharta (Dip)

Originally from Punjab, this yummy dip can be served as a very messy finger food. The deep plum coloured SuperFood aubergine is bursting with nutrients - vitamins A, C and B vitamins including folate. It also has anti-viral properties for cold and flu protection.

Pre-heat the oven to 200C/400F/gas mark 6. Place the aubergines on a baking tray and bake for 15-20mins until soft to the touch.

Whilst the aubergines are baking, heat the oil in a pot, add the onion and stir-fry on low heat for 3-4mins. Add the tomato, garlic, cumin, coriander, black pepper and stir-fry on medium heat until the water from the tomato has burnt away and is very soft.

Turn to low heat and add the yogurt a little at a time, stirring continuously to avoid curdling. Stir-fry for a further minute and set aside.

Once the aubergines are cooked and cooled, cut them in half lengthways and scoop out the flesh, it should be juicy and soft. Add the flesh to the pot with the cooked onion and tomato and combine. Mash or blend to achieve a textured paste. Serve to baby warm over wholemeal pitta bread strips.

Tip: the best way to cook an aubergine is to bake it. There's better flavour, it's juicier and for us mums hassle-free! Simply whack it in the oven, have a cuppa, and take it out when the oven bleeps.

4 baby aubergines/ eggplants - washed, pricked all around

1 tbsp olive oil

½ onion - peeled, chopped

1 tomato - washed, deseeded, chopped

½ tsp minced garlic

Pinch of ground cumin

Pinch of ground coriander

Pinch of ground black pepper

1 tbsp plain unsweetened yogurt

Banana and Cinnamon Roti Wrap

A roti (chapatti) wrap, also called a 'baaboro', was my favourite childhood snack. Made with my mum's soft, freshly cooked roti it was smeared with ghee, sprinkled with sugar, rolled and scoffed within a matter of minutes... it was delicious! Baby's version is just as delicious but far more nutritious; prepared using only naturally sweet fruit, and a complimentary sweet aromatic spice. See page 10 for full nutritional details.

Warm the roti (chapatti) on a large frying pan, in the microwave for 10-20secs or on a thava (round, flat frying pan), if you have one.

Once warmed, spread the butter or ghee evenly over the roti and lightly sprinkle the cinnamon over it. Add the banana slices in a row, roll up the roti and cut into bite-sized pieces for your little one.

Tip one: this five minute SuperMeal is also fabulous as a quick after school snack for older children.

Tip two: make this finger food suitable for Stage 2 babies by offering the slices of banana without the roti, and just a touch of cinnamon.

1 roti - homemade (page 88) or ready-made
1 tsp unsalted butter or ghee
Sprinkle of ground cinnamon
1 banana - peeled, sliced

Playdate Pizza Pitta Fingers

• •

Dried mixed herbs are fantastic! Thyme, parsley, oregano, sage and basil - some the most highly ranked SuperSpices all available in one handy bottle. This combination of herbs ensures your little one will receive vitamins A and K, iron, and anti-bacterial and anti-inflammatory protection, amongst other benefits; all sprinkled into a delicious tomato sauce base which is also rich in lycopene.

Tomato sauce base:

1 x 400g (14oz) tinned chopped tomatoes

1 tsp minced garlic

½ tsp dried mixed herbs

¼ tsp ground cumin

Pinch of ground black pepper

1 pack of 6 pittas – white or wholemeal

40g (1½oz) medium Cheddar cheese - grated

One serving:

1-2 tbsp tomato sauce base

1 pitta – white or wholemeal

Handful of medium Cheddar cheese – grated

Lay all of the pittas on a foil-covered baking tray and distribute the sauce evenly between all six. Then sprinkle over the cheese and place them under a hot grill until the cheese has melted and is bubbling. Remove from the grill, cut into long strips. Allow cooling before serving to baby and friends.

One serving: It is more convenient to cook up a big batch of tomato sauce base in one go rather than cooking it for one serving, so follow same method as above, and freeze the remaining sauce into individual servings (page 189).

Tip: add mushrooms, sweetcorn and bell peppers and transform this finger food into a quick and filling after school snack for older children.

Sweet SuperMeals

When describing Asian desserts the words:

Rich, luscious and indulgent come to mind.

A few other words come to mind too: unhealthy, sugary and saturated fats!

Nevertheless, knowing all too well how delicious Asian desserts are, I was not going to let Aaliyah miss out on these delights! So taste was definitely one of the biggest influences behind creating these wonderful puddings for her, and the other stemmed from 'my big fat family gatherings'. Whilst everyone indulged in mithai (sweets), gajar halwa, seviyan and more at family events, Aaliyah would sit and watch every mouthful her uncles, aunts and cousins devoured, completely mesmerised. I felt awful, like a Wicked Witch who wouldn't let her daughter enjoy these wonderful desserts.

So this chapter is dedicated to healthy adaptations of traditional Asian desserts exclusively for baby to indulge in. The words to describe these desserts are:

Energy-boosting, probiotic, fresh fruity goodness, naturally sweet and fibre-rich.

Being exceptionally nutritious, these desserts can also be served as healthy snacks, and for as long as your little one wants to enjoy them for. Aaliyah still adored these desserts at 18 months and beyond, so there really is no strict time frame on these recipes.

Bananaberry Raita

A delicious, naturally sweet fresh fruit raita that Aaliyah still adores! This one is a SuperFood and SuperSpice bonanza because every ingredient has amazing health benefits. Yogurt is probiotic and calcium-rich, the potassium (in bananas) works efficiently to aid calcium absorption leading to strong teeth and bones for baby. The blueberries add an extra boost of vitamin C and K, and the ginger keeps the digestive tract in healthy working order.

Place the banana and blueberries in a bowl, spoon in the yogurt and sprinkle over the ginger.

Mash the fruit with a spoon to create soft lumps for baby, and stir. The yogurt will change colour from white to a very subtle shade of purple courtesy of the blueberries.

Serve to baby as a dessert, or a healthy between meals snack.

1 banana - peeled, sliced

Handful of blueberries - fresh, washed, halved

2-3 tbsp plain unsweetened yogurt

Sprinkle of ground ginger

Classic Gajar Halwa

• •

Gajar Halwa, one of the most famous Indian desserts. The key ingredient being the SuperFood carrot, so you know this dish is bursting with beta-carotene goodness. Raisins too contain antioxidant power of their own, excellent for eye and bone health and for fighting bacteria in the mouth, protecting your little ones baby teeth from tooth decay. Since this delicious dessert is bursting with nutritional value, it can be served either as a snack or after meal treat.

Melt the butter or ghee in a pot, add the cardamom and carrots and stir-fry for 5mins.

Pour in the milk and add the cinnamon and raisins. Bring to the boil gradually on a low heat; this will take 5-10mins.

Simmer (uncovered) for 15mins, stirring occasionally until the mixture begins to thicken. Once all of the milk has been absorbed, remove from the heat. Serve to baby warm.

IMPORTANT: remove the cardamom pod before serving to baby.

1 tbsp unsalted butter or ghee

1 whole cardamom pod - green

2 medium carrots - peeled, washed, grated (in food processor)

150ml (5fl oz) of whole milk

Pinch of ground cinnamon

15g (½ oz) raisins - soaked in warm water (5mins), drained, chopped

Coconut Seviyan (Vermicelli Pudding)

Traditionally served as either breakfast or dessert, seviyan (vermicelli) is deliciously creamy. Made from very thin pasta, this dish is an excellent starchy food source for baby. The complex carbohydrates combined with the energy-boosting power of the coconut makes this a perfect slow release energy snack.

1 tbsp unsalted butter or ghee

40g (1½ oz) vermicelli

350ml (12fl oz) of whole milk

3 saffron strands

1 tbsp unsweetened desiccated coconut

15g (½ oz) raisins - soaked in warm water (5mins), drained, chopped

Melt the butter or ghee in a pot. Over the pot break the vermicelli with your hands into small pieces and toss in. Stir-fry lightly on low heat for 2-3mins until it turns golden brown.

Pour in the milk and add the saffron, coconut and raisins. Bring to the boil gradually on low heat; this will take 5-10mins. Simmer (uncovered) until the milk becomes creamy, but still remains fluid, stirring occasionally.

If the seviyan becomes too heavy, add some extra milk, stir and serve to baby warm. Delicious!

Creamy Sweet Potato Dream

This warm, sweet, aromatic delight is yummy and bursting with immune-boosting capabilities, supplied by the antioxidant beta-carotene (vitamin A), and lauric acid from the coconut milk.

1 medium sweet potato - peeled, washed, finely sliced

200ml (7fl oz) unsweetened coconut milk

150ml (5fl oz) of whole milk

Sprinkle of ground nutmeg

1 whole cardamom pod - green

Place the sweet potato slices in a layer at the base of a large pot. Continue to layer until all of the slices have been placed, and cover with coconut milk and whole milk.

Bring to the boil gradually on low heat; this will take 5-10mins. Then simmer (covered) for 10mins or until the potatoes are cooked thoroughly. Remove from the heat and mash. The milk will transform to light orange colour and the consistency should be quite runny. If not, add some extra milk.

Return to the heat adding the nutmeg, cardamom and stir. Simmer (uncovered) on low heat for a further 5-10mins until the milk thickens. Once cooked, serve to baby warm.

IMPORTANT: remove the cardamom pod before serving to baby.

Mint Yogurt Raita

It's not sweet I know, but seemed like the most appropriate place to put it!
Yogurt raitas are a common accompaniment to Indian dishes; they go together like fish and chips! For baby I created this savoury raita to add another layer of flavour to my curries and to get an extra probiotic boost into her diet. The 'good' bacteria from the yogurt combined with the digestive power of the mint, cumin and ginger, suggests healthy bowels all around.

Spoon the yogurt into a bowl and add the mint, cumin and ginger. Fold the aromatic spices into the yogurt until well combined. Serve alongside any of my curries in this book.

2 tbsp plain unsweetened yogurt
¼ tsp dried mint
Sprinkle of ground cumin
Sprinkle of ground ginger

Papaya Shrikhand (Yogurt)

A traditional sweet yogurt dessert chock-full of probiotic goodness, and contains the golden orange SuperFood Papaya. This exotic fruit is filled with antioxidant vitamins A (in the form of beta-carotene) and C. Both play a vital role in promoting a healthy immune system. Similarly rich in folate, this fruit will aid healthy growth. Only taking a few minutes to prepare, this is an effortless yogurt dessert.

½ tbsp of whole milk

2 saffron strands

4 tbsp plain unsweetened yogurt

½ ripe papaya - peeled, deseeded, cubed

Pinch of ground cardamom - green

In a cup pour the milk, warm for a few seconds in the microwave, add the saffron, stir and set aside. The warm milk will help the saffron to dissolve. When this happens the milk will slowly transform from white, to a light golden orange colour.

Next spoon the yogurt into a blender and add the papaya, cardamom and orange saffron milk. Blend until smooth, place in a small container and serve to baby.

Tip: also delicious prepared with mango, with the same beta-carotene goodness!

Saffron Date Kheer (Rice Pudding)

A luscious, creamy, gorgeous rice pudding! Even I've had a few sneaky mouthfuls of this one. Containing saffron the world's most expensive aromatic spice, it contains the compound 'crocin' - important for good memory and can actually help baby's ability to learn new and exciting things. Dates are also impressive, with antioxidant power close to that of blueberries, they are a concentrated source of calories (energy), are fibre-rich helping to keep bowels healthy, and are a wonderful source of minerals, potassium, selenium and calcium.

40g (1½oz) white basmati rice - washed, drained

550ml (1 pint) of whole milk

3 saffron strands

Sprinkle of ground cinnamon

15g (½oz) fresh dates - deseeded, finely chopped

Place the rice in a pot, pour in half of the milk and stir, you will need to save the other half for later.

Bring the milk to the boil gradually on low heat; this will take 5-10mins. Let it simmer (uncovered) until all of the milk has been absorbed by the rice. It will be thick and creamy.

Remove from the heat and mash the rice. Return to the heat and pour in the remaining milk. Add the saffron, cinnamon, dates and stir. Simmer (uncovered) on low heat until the milk and mashed rice have combined into a rich, gooey consistency. If the kheer becomes too heavy just add some extra milk and stir. Serve to baby warm as an after meal treat.

Apple and Pear Jardo (Sweet Rice)

• •

Growing up I've always loved this sweet rice dessert. The rice was cooked in tons of sugar and it was bright orange in colour! There really was nothing healthy about it, but it tasted amazing! However, in my reinvented version for baby, the sweet taste comes from the tender apple and pear chunks. Combined with the wholegrain goodness of brown rice, this jardo is chock-full of fibre and complex carbohydrates, providing your little one with lots of slow release energy to keep her playing for longer.

Heat the butter (or ghee) and oil in a pot on low heat and add the cinnamon and cardamom. Stir-fry for a minute then pour in the water, apple juice and add the rice. Bring to the boil and simmer (covered) for 35-40mins until all of the liquid has been absorbed and the rice is tender.

Whilst the rice is cooking, steam the apple and pear in a steamer or in the microwave by placing them in a microwavable dish and adding 2 tablespoons of water. Cover the dish with either a lid (leaving a small vent) or cling film (piercing a few holes), and steam on high for 1-1½mins until tender.

Once cooked, drain the excess water and add the fruit chunks to the cooked rice. Combine well. Serve to baby warm as a dessert or healthy snack... yummy!

IMPORTANT: remove the cardamom pod and cinnamon stick before serving to baby.

1 tbsp unsalted butter or ghee

1 tbsp vegetable oil

1 small cinnamon stick

1 whole cardamom pod - green

400ml (14fl oz) of water

100ml (3½fl oz) pure unsweetened apple juice

100g (3½oz) brown basmati rice - soaked in water (10mins) - washed, drained

½ sweet apple - peeled, cored, chopped

1 small firm pear - peeled, cored, chopped

Mango and Banana Lassi

Lassi, a scrumptious traditional yogurt-based drink typically loaded with sugar. Baby's version however is not, and is comparable to a fruit smoothie. As with banana, mango provides a vast range of health benefits including promoting good memory, eyesight and contains antioxidant vitamin E, which helps to speed up the healing of wounds and reduces scarring. Just what your little one will need when she starts taking tumbles.

Place the yogurt, mango and banana into a blender and blend until smooth. Pour into baby's drinking/ sippy cup and serve.

Alternative fruit lassi combinations include:

- Sweet Plum and Blueberry Lassi

- Papaya and Mango Lassi

- Strawberry and Raspberry Lassi

Feel free to get creative and try out new and exciting fruit combinations so you can tailor them specifically to your little one's taste buds.

4 tbsp plain unsweetened yogurt
½ ripe mango - peeled, cubed
½ banana - peeled, halved

Meat SuperMeals

By this stage your little one will be a **well-oiled 'chewing machine'.** This newly perfected skill will allow her to break down meat effectively, making it easier for her digestive system to process. So if you have already introduced meat into baby's diet, there is no longer any need to puree the meat before serving.

If you are just about to introduce meat however, it is important to know you should only use **lean cuts of meat**, as lots of fat will be difficult for baby to digest. Try to use the following cuts:

Chicken - skinless, breast portions
Turkey -skinless, breast portions
Lamb - stew/ casserole meat chunks or the foreshank, aka 'lamb shank'.
Beef - Top Sirloin or Eye of Round roast

When I embarked on Aaliyah's meat and poultry journey from the age of 10 months, I offered her lean minced meat meals to begin with — either chicken or lamb as the meat was already ground into tiny pieces. I then moved on to small tender chunks of meat shredding cooked chunks with my fingers before serving. As Aaliyah grew, I left them whole and she would shred or cut them herself.

At this stage I was also more confident with the food I was feeding Aaliyah. So these SuperMeals are **chunkier, include new spices**, and reflect the method in which big family meals are prepared; involving the use of many whole garam masalas - cloves, black peppercorns, cinnamon sticks and more, rather than restricting use to their ground counterparts.

IMPORTANT: you must ensure ALL meat and poultry has been thoroughly cooked to avoid food poisoning.

Classic Keema Curry

A mouth-watering traditional curry perfect as a first meat dish for baby. A great mixture of protein, starch and veggies, this curry is healthy and also versatile. Cook with lean minced chicken, lamb or beef to keep this curry interesting, as using different meats will alter the taste of this curry considerably.

2 tbsp olive oil

1 onion - peeled, chopped

1 whole clove

1 whole black peppercorn

1 small cinnamon stick

1 tsp minced ginger

1 tsp minced garlic

100g (3½oz) lean lamb, beef or chicken mince

1 tomato - washed, grated

½ tsp ground cumin

½ tsp ground coriander

¼ tsp ground turmeric

½ tbsp tomato puree

1 small white potato - peeled, washed, cubed

40g (1½oz) peas - frozen, washed

Heat the oil in a pot and add the onion, clove, peppercorn and cinnamon. Stir-fry on medium heat until the onion is golden. Add the ginger, garlic and stir-fry for a further 30secs-1min then add the mince and continue to stir-fry until the meat is sealed. Add the tomato, cumin, coriander, turmeric, tomato puree, stir-fry for a further minute, then turn to low heat, add a splash of water and simmer covered for 10-15mins or until the mince is thoroughly cooked.

While the mince is cooking, place the potato cubes in a microwavable dish and add 2 tablespoons of water. Cover the dish with either a lid (leaving a small vent) or cling film (piercing a few holes), and steam on high for 2-2½mins until tender. Drain and set aside.

Once the mince is cooked, add the peas to the pot, stir and continue to simmer covered for 2-3mins until the peas are tender. Switch off the hob, add the potato cubes and combine well. Serve to baby warm with roti and a dollop of plain yogurt. Delicious!

IMPORTANT: remove the clove, black peppercorn and cinnamon stick before serving to baby.

Chicken and Saag Pasanda

By far one of Aaliyah's favourite meals! The key to ensuring no nutrients are lost in this curry is to lightly steam the spinach. Spinach (saag) is a SuperFood abundant in vitamins and minerals containing vitamins A, K, folate, iron and carotenoids lutein and zeaxanthin, required for healthy vision. When teamed with chicken makes a fabulously nutritious curry. Chicken is not only protein-rich; it contains the mineral 'selenium' believed to be anti-cancer and regulates the hormones released by the thyroid gland, essential for weight control.

2 tbsp olive oil

1 onion - peeled, chopped

1 small cinnamon stick

½ tsp minced ginger

½ tsp minced garlic

1 chicken breast fillet (skinless) - cut into 1cm cubes

¼ tsp ground turmeric

150ml (5fl oz) of water

½ tsp ground garam masala

1 tbsp tomato puree

3 tbsp plain unsweetened yogurt

120g (4oz) spinach leaves- washed thoroughly, chopped (no stems)

Heat the oil in a pot, add the onion, cinnamon and stir-fry on medium-low heat for 3-4mins. Then add the ginger, garlic, chicken and turmeric. Stir-fry for a minute then turn to low heat, add the water, garam masala, tomato puree and the yogurt one spoon at a time, stirring in between to avoid curdling. Simmer (uncovered) on low heat for 8-10mins until the chicken is tender.

While the chicken is simmering, steam the spinach using a steamer or in the microwave by placing it in a microwavable dish (do not add extra water); cover the dish with either a lid (leaving a small vent) or cling film (piercing a few holes), and steam on high for 2½mins or until wilted. Then drain the excess water and set aside.

Once the chicken is tender, add the cooked spinach and combine well. Cut or shred the chicken cubes as necessary and serve with roti or overcooked rice.

IMPORTANT: remove the cinnamon stick before serving to baby.

Chicken Pilaf with Vegetables

Pilaf or Pulao, a traditional rice dish cooked with either vegetables, meat or both. Yogurt plays an important role in this dish acting as a wonderful substitute to salt by providing a sharp taste to the meal. When yogurt is cooked, the live, 'good' bacteria are killed by the high temperature. Nevertheless, yogurt is still a great source of calcium, potassium and protein. Another source of protein is the chicken rich in B vitamins (niacin and B6), both required to help convert food into energy.

1½ tbsp olive oil

1 onion - peeled, chopped

1 whole cardamom pod - black

1 whole clove

1 small cinnamon stick

1 tomato - washed, chopped

¼ tsp ground black pepper

1 tsp cumin seeds

1 tsp minced ginger

1 tsp of minced garlic

Squeeze of ½ a lemon - ensuring no seeds fall in

2 tbsp plain unsweetened yogurt

1 chicken breast fillet (skinless) - cut into 1cm cubes

100g (3½oz) white basmati rice - washed, drained

60g (2½oz) cauliflower florets - washed, chopped (no stems)

40g (1½oz) peas - frozen, washed

250ml (8fl oz) of water

Heat the oil in a pot and add the onion, cardamom, clove, and cinnamon. Stir-fry until the onion browns. Turn to low heat and add the tomato, black pepper, cumin, ginger, garlic, lemon juice and yogurt - one spoon at a time, stirring in between to avoid curdling. Then add the chicken and stir-fry for 5mins.

Add the rice and cauliflower to the pot, pour in the water, stir and bring to the boil. Simmer (covered) on low heat for 10-15mins until the rice is tender and all of the water has been absorbed.

While the rice is cooking, steam the peas in a steamer or in the microwave by placing them in a microwavable dish and adding 2 tablespoons of water. Cover the dish with either a lid (leaving a small vent) or cling film (piercing a few holes), and steam on high for 1-1½mins. Drain and set aside.

Once the rice is tender (it will look a little moist when it's done), add the peas, combine well, cover the pot and set aside for 5mins. Serve to baby warm.

IMPORTANT: remove the cardamom, clove and cinnamon stick before serving to baby.

Chunky Spaghetti Bolognaise

Aaliyah loved this SuperMeal, she slurped up the lot in record time! Containing the SuperFood apricot, this fruit is fibre-rich and loaded with beta-carotene. The bolognaise sauce also includes dried oregano, a SuperSpice containing one of the highest antioxidant levels compared to other SuperSpices (page 14). Oregano is also anti-bacterial and loaded with vitamin K, required for effective blood clotting to heal wounds and for building strong bones.

Heat the oil in a pot, add the onion and stir-fry on medium-low heat for 3-4mins until soft and golden. Add the garlic, ginger and stir-fry for 30secs-1min then add the mince along with the black pepper, garam masala, turmeric and stir-fry until sealed (opaque). Add the tomatoes and pour in half of the water, you will need to save the rest for later. Simmer (covered) on low heat for 5-6mins.

Finally add the carrot, courgette, apricots, oregano, tomato puree and the remaining water. Continue to simmer for a further 10mins until the mince and all of the vegetables are well-cooked.

One serving: Serve 2-3 heaped tablespoons of bolognaise sauce with 20g (¾oz) cooked spaghetti, broken into small pieces.

Save the remaining sauce by freezing it in individual servings (page 189). Then simply boil up enough spaghetti for one serving every time you take a bolognaise portion out from the freezer.

2 tbsp olive oil

1 onion - peeled, chopped

1 tsp minced garlic

½ tsp minced ginger

100g (3½oz) lean lamb, beef or chicken mince

Pinch of ground black pepper

½ tsp ground garam masala

¼ tsp ground turmeric

200g (7oz) tinned chopped tomatoes

200ml (7fl oz) of water

1 medium carrot - peeled, washed, grated

1 small courgette/ zucchini - washed, grated

30g (1oz) dried apricots - finely chopped

¼ tsp dried oregano

1 tbsp tomato puree

Garam Yorkshire Hotpot

A traditional slow-cooked meal originating from the north of England. This is a hearty hotpot with a little garam masala thrown in for difference. Loaded with iron for baby, this meal is delicious and nutritious.

Pre-heat oven to 160C/ 325F/ gas mark 3.

Melt the butter in a frying pan and add the lamb and flour. Stir-fry continuously until the lamb pieces have browned. Then remove and place in a small oven-proof dish.

Using the same frying pan heat a little oil and add the onion, carrot, bay leaf and stir-fry until the onion is soft and golden. Add the garlic and garam masala to the pan and stir-fry for a further 30secs, then immediately pour the mixture over the lamb in the ovenproof dish followed by the stock. Place the potato slices in a layer over the top until it forms a cover for the stew underneath.

Brush a little melted butter or oil over the potato slices, cover the dish loosely with foil and place on the middle shelf of the oven and slow cook for 1½ hours.

Allow cooling and shred or mash the meal as necessary for baby. For older children serve with a side of freshly cooked vegetables for a more filling meal. Delicious!

25g (1 oz) unsalted butter

100g (3½oz) lean lamb cubes – boneless, fat-trimmed, cut into 1cm pieces

Sprinkle of plain flour

½ onion – peeled, chopped

1 medium carrot – peeled, washed, shredded

1 bay leaf

¼ tsp minced garlic

¼ tsp ground garam masala

60ml (2½fl oz) lamb stock – baby-friendly

1 white potato – peeled, washed, sliced

Coconut Chicken Curry

This SuperMeal is bursting with immune strengthening ingredients. Fresh lemon and broccoli provide vitamin C, and the coconut provides a source of anti-viral fats to keep cold and flu viruses at bay. In addition the chicken is anti-cancer and is an excellent source of 'essential' amino acids (protein), required for healthy growth and development.

1½ tbsp olive oil

1 onion - peeled, chopped

1 chicken breast fillet (skinless) - cut into 1cm cubes

¼ tsp ground turmeric

1 tomato - washed, grated

½ tsp minced garlic

¼ tsp ground cumin

150ml (5fl oz) unsweetened coconut milk

1 tbsp unsweetened desiccated coconut

Squeeze of ½ a lemon - ensuring no seeds fall in

¼ tsp ground garam masala

60g (2½oz) broccoli florets - washed, chopped (no stems)

Heat the oil in a pot, add the onion and stir-fry on medium-low heat for 3-4mins until soft and golden. Add the chicken, turmeric and stir-fry until the chicken is sealed (opaque). Add the tomato, garlic, cumin and continue to stir-fry for a further 2-3mins.

Add the coconut milk, desiccated coconut, lemon juice, garam masala and simmer on low heat for a further 10mins, stirring occasionally until the chicken is tender. If at any point the curry looks dry, add a little extra water and continue to simmer.

Whilst the chicken is simmering, steam the broccoli in a steamer or in the microwave by placing it in a microwavable dish and adding 2 tablespoons of water. Cover the dish with either a lid (leaving a small vent) or cling film (piercing a few holes), and steam on high for 1½-2mins until tender. Once cooked, drain the excess water and add to the curry at the end. Combine well and serve to baby warm with roti or overcooked rice.

Fruity Lamb Tagine

A heavenly tagine so delicious I've made a family size portion and served it up as a main meal. Incredibly easy to make, protein-rich and abundant in vitamins and minerals, this tagine is a real gem. Containing paprika, a vibrant red SuperSpice that aids baby's ability to absorb the iron found in lamb. Other nutrients include antioxidant beta-carotene from the apricots, antioxidant lycopene from the tomatoes, and various other anti-viral and immune-boosting compounds.

1 tbsp olive oil

1 onion - peeled, chopped

1 tsp minced garlic

200g (7oz) lean lamb (boneless) - cut into 1cm cubes

Sprinkle of plain flour

200g (7oz) tinned chopped tomatoes

450ml (15fl oz) vegetable or lamb stock - baby-friendly

Squeeze of ½ a lemon - ensuring no seeds fall in

1 small cinnamon stick

½ tsp ground cumin

½ tsp ground coriander

¼ tsp ground black pepper

½ tsp ground paprika

½ tsp ground ginger

20g (¾ oz) raisins

50g (2oz) dried apricots - finely chopped

1 firm pear - washed, peeled, cored, sliced

Heat the oil in a large pot, add the onion, garlic and stir-fry on medium-low heat until the onion is soft and golden. Then add the lamb, flour and stir-fry for a few minutes until the lamb has browned.

Pour in the tomatoes, stock, lemon juice and add all the spices (cinnamon, cumin, coriander, black pepper, paprika, ginger), and all of the fruit (raisins, apricots, pear). Bring to the boil and simmer (covered) on low heat for 1½ hours. If at any point the tagine looks dry, add a little extra water, cover and continue to simmer until melt-in-the-mouth tender. Serve to baby warm with cous cous, overcooked rice.

IMPORTANT: remove the cinnamon stick before serving to baby.

Snuggly Chicken and Vermicelli Soup

Chicken soup - a home remedy used to soothe cold and flu symptoms for generations. So when Aaliyah had a cold, I felt compelled to rustle up some chicken soup to make her feel better. This soup contains cold and flu fighting SuperSpices - cloves, cumin, cardamom and turmeric. It also includes immune-boosting vitamin A (from beta-carotene in carrots), vitamin C (sweetcorn), and provides starch for energy (vermicelli). A tasty way to help replace lost fluids, soothe sore throats, and make your little one feel snuggly and warm inside.

Heat the oil in a pot, add the onions, cloves, cardamom and stir-fry on medium-low heat for 3-4mins until the onions are golden. Add the garlic and stir-fry for 30secs-1min followed by the chicken, turmeric, black pepper, cumin and cook for a further 5-8mins.

Pour in the stock, add the carrot, sweet corn and over the pot, break the vermicelli into small pieces with your hands and toss in. Bring to the boil and simmer (uncovered) on medium-low heat for 6-8mins until the veggies, chicken and vermicelli are tender. Serve to baby warm on its own or with soft brown bread as a more filling meal.

IMPORTANT: remove the cloves and cardamom pod before serving to baby.

1 tbsp olive oil

½ onion - peeled, chopped

2 whole cloves

1 whole cardamom pod - black

1 tsp minced garlic

1 chicken breast fillet (skinless) - cut into 1cm cubes

¼ tsp ground turmeric

Pinch of ground black pepper

½ tsp ground cumin

550ml (1 pint) hot chicken or vegetable stock - baby-friendly

1 medium carrot - peeled, washed, diced

75g (3oz) tinned sweet corn (no added salt) - drained

25g (1oz) vermicelli

Mum's Lamb Curry with Sweet Potato

• •

Lamb... my favourite red meat. When slow-cooked in curry it absorbs all of the gorgeous aromatic spices and melts-in-the-mouth. Lamb is an excellent source of essential amino acids (protein), essential omega 3 fatty acids, selenium, iron and zinc necessary for good taste and smell senses. Combined with the benefits of beta-carotene (vitamin A) from the sweet potato, this is a wonderfully nutritious meal for baby.

Heat the oil in a pot and add the onion, cloves, cinnamon, peppercorns, cardamom and stir-fry on medium-low heat for 3-4mins.

Then add the lamb, ginger, garlic, turmeric and continue to stir-fry until the lamb is sealed (opaque). Add the tomatoes, cumin, coriander, paprika, lemon juice, water and yogurt. Bring to the boil and simmer (covered) for 1½ hours, or until the lamb is tender, stirring occasionally. If at any point the curry looks dry, add a little water.

Whilst the curry is simmering, steam the sweet potato in either a steamer or in the microwave by placing it in a microwavable dish and adding 2 tablespoons of water. Cover the dish with either a lid (leaving a small vent) or cling film (piercing a few holes), and steam on high for 4-5mins until tender. Once cooked, drain the excess water and add to the curry at the end. Combine well and serve to baby warm with roti or overcooked rice.

IMPORTANT: remove the cloves, cinnamon stick, peppercorns and cardamom pod before serving to baby.

2 tbsp olive oil

1 onion - peeled, chopped

2 whole cloves

1 small cinnamon stick

2 whole black peppercorns

1 whole cardamom pod - black

200g (7oz) lean lamb (boneless) - cut into 1cm cubes

½ tsp minced ginger

1 tsp minced garlic

¼ tsp ground turmeric

200g (7oz) tinned chopped tomatoes

½ tsp ground cumin

½ tsp ground coriander

¼ tsp ground paprika

A few drops of fresh lemon - ensuring no seeds fall in

350ml (12fl oz) of water

1 tbsp plain unsweetened yogurt

1 small sweet potato - washed, peeled, cubed

Family SuperMeals

Congratulations! Now that your little one is a **spice connoisseur** she has graduated on to Stage 4 - Family SuperMeals! This is what we've been training for!

There is no longer any need to cook separate family meals, so this chapter is about adapting your recipes ensuring **one meal is suitable for the whole family!** And there is still no-added salt, sugar or chillies in your little ones meals.

"When is the best time to introduce chillies?" I hear you ask... Well there is no strict rule about this. I would suggest introducing chillies when you feel your little one is ready for the challenge. This could be anywhere between 18 months to two years or later. When I was a child, I was eating the same heat as the rest of the family when I was just two! So it really depends on your little one's taste buds.

When you do begin, however, I would recommend starting with a mild chilli powder and introducing just a small pinch. Once your little one is comfortable eating this level of heat, increase this gradually to a quarter teaspoon, then half a teaspoon and slowly transfer over to a hotter chilli powder. Use the same process as before – using just a pinch to begin with, and continue until your little one is eating the same heat as the rest of the family.

Avoid fresh green chillies altogether until your little one is 100 percent comfortable with red chilli powder, as fresh green chillies are extremely hot, hot, hot!

Toddler Eating Habits — What to Expect

Between the ages of 12 to 18 months, you'll notice your little one's motor skills will be further advanced making her more independent, and so she'll be feeding herself with a spoon as well as using her hands. This newly found independence will also make her aware that she has a choice over what she eats, potentially causing mayhem at meal times.

In these situations I found family meal times were great! Toddlers learn new behaviour by imitating what parents, siblings and peers do, so family meal times encouraged Aaliyah to eat nutritious meals as she was eating the same food as the rest of the family. Setting her place at the dinner table was also great for making her feel recognised as a small 'grown-up' and an integral part of the family, which again encouraged her to eat her food.

Don't get me wrong, this was by no means the answer to every mother's eternal burning question… "How do I coax my little one into eating all of her food?" I still experienced difficult meal times whereby I desperately tried to persuade Aaliyah to eat her dinner, and she was more interested in decorating the floor with it. But it did play a role in reducing the amount of stressful mealtimes I experienced.

Another technique which encouraged Aaliyah to eat at mealtimes was involving her in our weekly shopping trips. As I'd wheel her around the supermarket in the shopping trolley, I'd ask her which fruit and vegetables we should buy. When she pointed out what she wanted, I allowed her to hold them for a while before she attempted to drop them on the floor, or whirl around and drop them behind her in the trolley. I found this worked really well for my little madam's independence as she felt involved in the decision making process.

Don't be alarmed if your little one appears to be eating less food. Within the first year babies experience rapid growth, however, when they reach toddlerhood their growth tends to slow down so the amount they eat will reflect this.

Also try not to get too stressed at meal times. It may appear that your little one has barely eaten one grain of rice, but toddlers will never let themselves go hungry. So switch off the TV and enjoy your family meals together. They are a time to eat healthy, tasty food, and to connect with the rest of the family. Building precious moments that should be enjoyed and cherished for years to come.

Tip: when eating a meal together your little one may prefer to steal food from your plate rather than eat her own. In this situation put some of her food on your plate. When she tries to swipe your food, she will happily munch on her own thinking she is eating mummy or daddy's.

Aloo Gobi

White SuperFoods are the main ingredients in this curry. Cauliflower (gobi), potatoes (aloo), ginger and garlic are all high in antioxidant activity. Cauliflower is high in vitamin C, great for healthy skin, brain function and immune system. Along with potatoes is also a great source of potassium, essential for keeping our internal organs in good working condition.

2 tbsp olive oil

1 onion - peeled, chopped

1 tsp cumin seeds

1½ tsp minced garlic

1 tsp minced ginger

1 tsp ground coriander

½ tsp ground garam masala

¼ tsp ground turmeric

2 medium white potatoes - peeled, washed, cubed

200ml (7fl oz) of water

400g (14oz) cauliflower florets - washed, chopped

Salt to taste (optional)

Red chilli powder to taste (optional)

Fresh coriander/ cilantro for garnish - washed

Heat the oil in a pot, add the onion and stir-fry until soft and golden. Add the cumin seeds, garlic, ginger, coriander, garam masala, turmeric and stir-fry for 30secs-1min to lightly cook the spices.

Add the potatoes, water and simmer (covered) on medium-low heat for 5mins. Then add the cauliflower, an extra splash of water, cover and continue to simmer for 10-15mins until both are tender.

Remove a serving for your little one and set aside. Then add salt and red chilli powder to the main pot and stir. Return to the heat for a further 1-2mins to lightly cook the chilli if you wish.

Garnish the main serving (and your little ones) with fresh coriander/ cilantro and serve with roti or naan.

Bhindi Masala Curry

Bhindi (okra or lady fingers), is a popular vegetable amongst South Asian cuisine, however, if prepared incorrectly can be quite slimy and unpleasant in texture. The best method to avoid this 'slime' is by lightly frying the bhindi before tossing it in with the curry sauce. Bhindi is rich in antioxidant vitamins A, C, E and vitamin K, essential for forming blood clots (scabs) to heal cuts and wounds, and is wonderful for strengthening bones.

400g (14oz) bhindi/ lady fingers/ okra - washed, chopped

50ml (2fl oz) olive oil

1 onion - peeled, chopped

1½ tsp minced garlic

½ tsp ground cumin

½ tsp ground coriander

¼ tsp ground turmeric

1 tsp ground paprika

200g (7oz) tinned chopped tomatoes

Squeeze of ½ a lemon - ensuring no seeds fall in

Salt to taste (optional)

Red chilli powder to taste (optional)

Drizzle olive oil in a large non-stick frying pan and lightly fry the bhindi on medium-low heat until they have browned slightly, and the slimy texture has gone. Remove from the pan, place on a paper towel and set aside. Cook the bhindi in two batches if necessary.

Using the same frying pan add the 50ml of oil, onions and stir-fry on medium heat until the onions have browned. This will make a rich curry sauce.

Add garlic, cumin, coriander, turmeric, paprika and stir-fry for a further 30secs-1min, then pour in the tomatoes and lemon juice. Simmer uncovered for 2-3mins. Then add the bhindi to the masala, stir and simmer on low heat for a further 2-3mins.

Once cooked, remove a serving for your little one and set aside. Add salt and red chilli powder to the main pot and stir. Return to the heat for a further 1-2mins.

Serve with roti as a main dish, or alongside my Lamb Rogan Josh (page 162) as a side dish. Delicious!

Butternut Chickpea Curry

Chickpeas, members of the protein-rich food group are an excellent source of fibre, folate and manganese - required for healthy brain function. Combined with the SuperFood health benefits of the butternut squash (antioxidant beta-carotene), this is a sweet, tangy curry the whole family will reap the health rewards from!

- 50ml (2fl oz) olive oil
- 1 onion - peeled, chopped
- 2 tsp minced garlic
- 1 tsp ground cumin
- ¼ tsp ground turmeric
- 1 tsp ground paprika
- 1 tbsp tomato puree
- ¼ tsp ground black pepper
- 1 x 400g (14oz) tinned chopped tomatoes
- 1 x 400g (14oz) tinned chickpeas - drained, washed
- 1 butternut squash - peeled, deseeded, cubed
- 250ml (8fl oz) of water
- Salt to taste (optional)
- Ground cayenne pepper to taste (optional)
- Fresh coriander/ cilantro for garnish - washed

Heat the oil in a pot, add the onion and stir-fry on medium-low heat until soft and golden. Add the garlic and stir-fry for 30secs - 1min then add the cumin, turmeric, paprika, tomato puree, black pepper and stir-fry for another minute to lightly cook the spices. Add the tomatoes, squash and pour in the water. Bring to the boil and simmer (covered) on a medium-low heat for 15mins.

Then add the chickpeas, stir and simmer for a further 5mins until the squash is tender. Once cooked, remove a serving for your little one and set aside.

Add salt and cayenne pepper to the main pot and stir. Return to the heat for a further 1-2mins. Garnish the main serving (and your little ones) with fresh coriander/ cilantro and serve with cous cous or rice.

Tip: tinned chickpeas are already cooked so there is no need to overcook them in the pot. Simply allow them to warm up and absorb the delicious flavours from the curry.

Tarka Coconut Dhal

This dhal requires the cooking technique 'tarka' or 'baghaar' whereby spices are intensely stir-fried in hot oil for a couple of minutes and poured over the dhal to give a strong burst of flavour. The dhal is also chock-full of healthy fats, fibre, protein, iron, and tastes extra yummy when eaten alongside my Masala Fish Curry (page 170); a match made in heaven!

Dhal: Heat the oil in a pot, add the onion, garlic, tomato and stir-fry on medium-low heat until the tomato is soft. Add the lentils, coconut milk, water and turmeric. Bring to the boil and simmer (uncovered) on medium-low heat for 15- 20mins until the lentils are tender. Once cooked, remove a serving for your little one and set aside. Add salt and red chilli powder to the main pot and stir.

Tarka/ Bhagaar: Just before serving, heat the oil in a frying pan, add the mustard seeds and stir-fry on medium-high heat until they begin to pop. Then add the onion, tomato and curry leaves. Continue to stir-fry for 2mins then add a teaspoon of the tarka to your little ones serving and combine well.

Add green chillies to the remaining tarka and stir-fry for another minute before placing on top of the main family dhal. Combine well and serve with rice or roti.

Dhal:

2 tbsp olive oil

½ onion - peeled, chopped

1 tsp minced garlic

½ tomato - washed, chopped

170g (6oz) red lentils - soaked in water (10mins), washed, drained

250ml (8fl oz) unsweetened coconut milk

300ml (½ pint) of water

¼ tsp ground turmeric

Salt to taste (optional)

½ tsp red chilli powder (optional)

Tarka/ Baghaar:

1 tbsp olive oil

1 tsp brown mustards seeds

½ onion - peeled, chopped

½ tomato - washed, chopped

6-8 curry leaves

3-4 fresh green chillies - stem removed, washed, pounded to paste

Matter Paneer

A South Asian vegetarian classic, matter (peas) and paneer, a commonly used unsalted full-fat Indian cottage cheese. Once only available in specialist Indian grocers, is now readily available at most supermarkets. Paneer is protein-rich and an excellent source of calcium, essential for building strong teeth and bones.

Drizzle olive oil in a large non-stick frying pan and lightly fry the paneer on medium-low heat until the cubes turn golden. Remove from the pan, place on a paper towel and set aside.

Using the same frying pan, add the 50ml of oil, cumin seeds, garlic and stir-fry on medium-low heat. When they begin to splutter add the tomatoes and stir-fry for 2-3mins. Then add the turmeric, water, tomato puree and allow the sauce to simmer on medium heat for a few minutes until the sauce thickens.

Once cooked, add the paneer, peas, stir and simmer for 2-3mins until the peas are tender, stirring occasionally.

Remove a serving for your little one and set aside. Then add salt and red chilli powder to the main pot and stir. Return to the heat for a further 1-2mins to lightly cook the chilli if you wish. Serve with roti.

225g (8oz) paneer - cubed

50ml (2fl oz) olive oil

1 tsp cumin seeds

1 tsp minced garlic

3 tomatoes - washed, chopped

¼ tsp ground turmeric

100ml (3½fl oz) of water

1 tbsp tomato puree

225g (8oz) peas - frozen, washed

Salt to taste (optional)

Red chilli powder to taste (optional)

Simple Family Dhal

I love serving dhal (lentils) to my family. Good for the heart, high in iron and due to its high-fibre nature helps to regulate blood sugar levels by providing slow-burning energy. This family dhal is also quick, easy to prepare, and is a perfect accompaniment to any veggie or meat curries.

2 tbsp olive oil

1 onion - peeled, chopped

1 tsp brown mustard seeds

1 tomato - washed, chopped

¼ tsp ground turmeric

1½ tsp cumin seeds

2 tsp minced garlic

1½ tsp minced ginger

170g (6oz) red lentils - soaked in water (10mins), washed, drained

4 bay leaves

750ml (1¼ pint) of water

Salt to taste (optional)

Red chilli powder to taste (optional)

Heat the oil in a pot, add the onion and stir-fry until soft and golden. Add the mustard seeds, tomato, turmeric, cumin seeds, garlic, ginger and stir-fry for a further 2mins. Add the lentils, bay leaves and pour in the water. Bring to the boil and simmer (covered) on medium-low heat for 15-20mins until the lentils are tender.

Once cooked, remove a serving for your little one and set aside. Then add salt and red chilli powder to the main pot and stir. Return to the heat for a further 1-2mins to lightly cook the chilli if you wish, although isn't necessary. Garnish with freshly chopped coriander/cilantro and serve with roti or rice.

Big and Small Kofta Curry

The name of this kofta (meatball) curry was inspired by one of Aaliyah's favourite children's TV shows at the time, and for obvious reasons - big kofta are for adults and older children, smaller kofta are for toddlers. Make these kofta with whichever lean minced meat of your choosing, either way they will be precious balls of protein-rich goodness.

Kofta: In a bowl add the mince, garlic, all of the spices and combine well. Remove 100g (3½oz) serving for baby and roll into 1cm balls. Set aside. Then add the green chillies and salt to the remaining mince and combine well. Roll into larger balls and set aside.

Curry Sauce: Heat the oil in a large pot, add the onion, cloves, peppercorns, cinnamon, cardamom and stir-fry on medium until the onions are browning. Then add the ginger, garlic, remaining spices and stir-fry for a few seconds before adding the tomatoes. Stir and cook the sauce for a few minutes, then turn to low heat and add all of the kofta balls gently. Simmer (covered) on low heat for 20-25mins until the kofta are thoroughly cooked. Stirring gently half way through.

Once cooked, remove the small kofta balls along with some sauce and set aside. Add salt and red chilli powder to the main pot and stir. Garnish with freshly chopped coriander/ cilantro and serve with roti or naan and a dollop of plain yogurt.

IMPORTANT: ensure there are no whole garam masalas included within baby's serving.

Koftas:

500g (1lb 2oz) chicken/ lamb mince

2 tsp minced garlic

1½ tsp ground garam masala

1 tsp ground cumin

½ tsp ground turmeric

4 green chillies – pounded (optional)

1 tsp salt (optional)

Curry sauce:

75ml (3fl oz) olive oil

1 onion - peeled, chopped

2 whole cloves, black peppercorns and cinnamon sticks

1 whole cardamom pod - black

½ tsp each of minced ginger/ garlic

¼ tsp ground turmeric

¾ tsp each of ground cumin/ coriander

1 tsp ground paprika

1 x 400g (14oz) tinned chopped tomatoes

Salt to taste (optional)

Red chilli powder to taste (optional)

Cardamom Chicken Curry

Cooking a whole chicken (on the bone) gives this curry a unique flavour that cannot be replicated by using a chicken breast fillet. It really is scrumptious. Cardamom is the main SuperSpice of this meal providing a multitude of vitamins and minerals. Rich in potassium, manganese, iron and niacin (also found in chicken), cardamom is the little pod with big health benefits.

Heat the oil in a pot and add the cardamom pods, onion, ginger, garlic, curry leaves and stir-fry on medium heat until the onions are golden brown. Add the turmeric, coriander, black pepper and stir-fry for a few seconds, followed by the tomatoes, tomato puree and water. Simmer (uncovered) for 10mins until the sauce becomes thick. Pop in the chicken pieces, add a little extra water if required and simmer (covered) on low heat for 20-25mins until the chicken is tender and the sauce is creamy.

Remove a serving of 1-2 chicken pieces for your little one, including at least one piece of darker meat such as the leg, as darker meat contains more iron. Add green chillies, salt and red chilli powder to the main pot and stir. Return to the heat for a further 1-2mins to lightly cook the chilli if you wish. Garnish the main serving (and your little ones) with fresh coriander/ cilantro and serve with roti, naan or rice.

IMPORTANT: ensure there are no cardamom pods included within baby's serving.

75ml (3fl oz) olive oil

6 whole cardamom pods - green, split

1 onion - peeled, chopped

1 tsp minced ginger

1½ tsp minced garlic

8-10 curry leaves

½ tsp ground turmeric

1 tsp ground coriander

¼ tsp ground black pepper

450g (1lb) tomatoes - washed, chopped

1 tbsp tomato puree

150ml (5fl oz) of water

1 whole chicken (skinless) - cut into 8 pieces, fat trimmed

3 green chillies - pounded (optional)

Salt to taste (optional)

Red chilli powder to taste (optional)

Fresh coriander/ cilantro for garnish – washed

Indian Cottage Pie

Smooth, creamy, classic British pie with an Indian twist. Containing Worcestershire sauce, my initial thought was 'there can't be any nutritional value in this condiment'. But I was utterly wrong! Worcestershire sauce is actually a source of 10 vitamins and minerals made using a mixture of ingredients rich in vitamin B6 (garlic, cloves and molasses), all excellent for building red blood cells. Another major ingredient is the oily fish anchovies which is a source of niacin required for a healthy nervous system.

Mash: Place the potatoes in a large pot, cover with water, bring to the boil and simmer (uncovered) until tender. Drain and mash. Then heat the milk and butter, add to the mashed potatoes along with the black pepper. Combine until smooth and creamy and set aside.

Pie filling: Heat the oil in a large frying pan, add the onion, cardamom and stir-fry until the onions are golden. Add the garlic, ginger, all of the spices and stir-fry for 30secs-1min before adding the mince. Stir-fry until browned then add the water, Worcestershire sauce, tomatoes, tomato puree, carrots, stir and bring to the boil. Simmer (covered) on medium-low heat for 15-20mins then remove the cardamom pods and allow cooling.

Pre-heat the oven to 180C/350F/gas mark 4. Remove a serving of mince for baby and place in a ramekin dish. Top with the mashed potatoes and set aside.

Add salt and cayenne pepper to the main pot, stir and spoon into a large over-proof dish. Top with the remaining mashed potatoes. Place both dishes in the oven and bake for 30-35mins. Allow cooling before serving. Delicious served with a side salad.

Mash:
4 white potatoes - peeled, cubed
150ml (5fl oz) of whole milk
2 tbsp unsalted butter
¼ tsp ground black pepper

Pie Filling:
50ml (2fl oz) olive oil
1 onion - peeled, chopped
2 whole cardamom pods - black
2 tsp each of minced garlic/ ginger
2 tsp ground coriander
1½ tsp ground cumin
½ tsp ground black pepper
450g (1lb) lean minced beef
50ml (2fl oz) of water
2 tbsp Worcestershire sauce
200g (7oz) tinned chopped tomatoes
1 tbsp tomato puree
2 medium carrots - peeled, diced
Salt to taste (optional)
Ground cayenne pepper (optional)

Indo-Moroccan Lamb Stew

· ·

A delectable, iron and protein-rich stew enhanced by the gorgeous flavours and health benefits of the SuperSpices: coriander, cinnamon, black pepper and garam masala. Containing antioxidant honey, this natural sweetener is anti-inflammatory, anti-viral and anti-bacterial, so excellent for treating cold and flu symptoms.

2 tbsp olive oil

1 onion - peeled, chopped

500g (1lb 2oz) lean lamb (boneless) - cubed

2 tsp minced garlic

550ml (1 pint) hot lamb or chicken stock - low salt

2 small cinnamon sticks

1 tsp clear runny honey

2 tsp ground garam masala

2 tsp ground coriander

½ tsp ground black pepper

80g (3oz) dried apricots – finely chopped

7g (¼oz) fresh mint leaves -roughly chopped

25g (1oz) ground almonds

Heat the oil in a large pot, add the onion, lamb, garlic and stir-fry on medium heat until the lamb has browned. Add the stock, cinnamon sticks, honey, garam masala, coriander, black pepper and stir. Bring to the boil and simmer (covered) on low heat for 1 hour, stirring occasionally. Then add the apricots, half of the mint, and ground almonds to thicken the sauce. Continue to simmer (covered) for 30mins until the lamb is melt-in-the-mouth tender.

Garnish the main serving (and your little ones) with the remaining mint leaves and serve with cous cous or rice.

Personally, I don't think this dish requires any extra salt, however if you would like to add some, remove a serving for your little one before adding any to the main pot and stir.

Lamb Rogan Josh

Found on the menu of virtually every Indian restaurant, this curry is delicious and flavoursome. The green bell pepper adds some healthy greenery to this meal making it rich in antioxidant vitamin C, lutein and zeaxanthin, as well as iron and protein.

75ml (3fl oz) olive oil

2 small cinnamon sticks

4 whole black peppercorns

4 whole cardamom pods - green, split

3 whole cloves

1 onion - peeled, chopped

2 tsp minced garlic

1½ tsp minced ginger

1 tsp cumin seeds

1 tsp ground coriander

2 tsp ground paprika

100g (3½oz) plain unsweetened yogurt

450g (1lb) lean lamb (boneless) - cubed

350ml (12fl oz) of water

1½ tbsp tomato puree

1 green bell pepper - washed, deseeded, diced

¼ tsp ground garam masala

Salt to taste (optional)

Ground cayenne pepper (optional)

Heat the oil in a pot and add the cinnamon, peppercorns, cardamom and cloves. Stir-fry on medium-low heat until they begin to sizzle, then add the onion and stir-fry until golden. Add the garlic, ginger, cumin seeds, coriander and paprika and stir-fry for a minute.

Turn to low heat add a splash of water and add the yogurt, a little at a time, stirring continuously to avoid curdling. Then add the lamb and cook until the lamb is sealed (opaque).

Add the water, tomato puree, stir and bring to the boil. Simmer (covered) on low heat for 1 hour 20mins. Then pop in the green bell pepper, stir and continue to simmer (covered) for 8-10mins until tender. Once cooked, remove a serving for your little one and set aside.

Sprinkle the garam masala, salt and cayenne pepper over the main pot and stir. Garnish the main serving (and your little ones) with fresh coriander/ cilantro and serve with roti, rice or naan.

IMPORTANT: ensure there are no whole garam masalas included within baby's serving.

Lamb, Saag and Aloo Curry

A scrummy curry containing the nutritional Superhero spinach (saag)! In addition to being rich in vitamin A (for a healthy immune system, skin and eyes), vitamin K (for healthy nervous system and strong bones), it is also anti-inflammatory, anti-cancer and rich in iron. Lamb is however the best source of iron and is also bursting with essential amino acids, necessary to keep our entire bodies in excellent working condition.

Heat the oil in a large pot and layer the onion, cloves, cardamom, peppercorns and cumin at the bottom, followed by the lamb, garlic, ginger and turmeric. Simmer (covered) on low heat for 10mins. Add the tomatoes, water, paprika, coriander, tomato puree and stir. Bring to the boil and simmer (covered) on low heat for 1½ hours stirring occasionally.

Whilst the lamb is cooking, steam the potato in either a steamer or in the microwave by placing it in a microwavable dish and adding 2 tablespoons of water. Cover the dish with either a lid (leaving a small vent) or cling film (piercing a few holes), and steam on high for 3-4mins or until tender. Drain and set aside. Next, steam the spinach for 2½mins or until wilted using the same method, DO NOT add any water. Drain set aside.

Once the lamb is tender, add the cooked spinach and potato. Combine well, remove a serving for your little one. Add salt and red chilli powder to the main pot and stir. Serve with naan, roti or rice.

IMPORTANT: ensure there are whole garam masalas included within baby's serving.

50ml (2fl oz) olive oil

1 onion - peeled, chopped

3 whole cloves

2 whole cardamom pods - black

4 whole black peppercorns

1 tsp cumin seeds

450g (1lb) lean lamb (boneless) - cubed

2 tsp minced garlic

1 tsp minced ginger

¼ tsp ground turmeric

1 x 400g (14oz) tinned chopped tomatoes

250ml (8fl oz) of water

1 tsp ground paprika

1½ tsp ground coriander

1 tbsp tomato puree

1 medium white potato - washed, peeled, cubed

300g (11oz) spinach leaves – washed thoroughly, chopped (no stems)

Salt to taste (optional)

Red chilli powder to taste (optional)

Mum's Chicken Karahi

• •

My mum's chicken karahi is a favourite meal of mine. My mouth waters at the mere thought of eating it, yummy! So, needless to say it had to make an appearance in this book. The powerful antioxidant lycopene makes a double appearance in this curry from the chopped tomatoes and tomato puree, helping to keep cancer, heart disease, and diabetes at bay.

Heat the oil in a pot, add the onions and stir-fry until soft and golden. Add the garlic, ginger and stir-fry for 30secs-1min, followed by the turmeric, cumin, coriander, paprika. Stir-fry for a few seconds more then add the add the tomatoes, tomato puree, stir and simmer (uncovered) on low heat until the sauce begins to thicken.

Add the chicken and simmer on medium-low heat for 10-15mins until the chicken is tender, stirring occasionally.

Once cooked, remove a serving for your little one and set aside. Add salt and red chilli powder to the main pot and stir. Return to the heat for a further 1-2mins to lightly cook the chilli if you wish.

Garnish the main serving (and your little ones) with fresh coriander/ cilantro and serve with rice or roti.

Tip: chicken breast doesn't take long to cook, so keep an eye on this curry as overcooking the fillets can lead to tough meat.

75ml (3fl oz) olive oil

1 onion - peeled, chopped

2 tsp minced garlic

1½ tsp minced ginger

½ tsp ground turmeric

1 tsp ground cumin

1 tsp ground coriander

2 tsp ground paprika

300g (11oz) tinned chopped tomatoes

1 tbsp tomato puree

2 chicken breast fillets (skinless) - cubed

Salt to taste (optional)

Red chilli powder to taste (optional)

Fresh coriander/ cilantro for garnish – washed

Paprika Salmon Linguine

A super quick creamy pasta dish rich with vitamin A and calcium from the double cream. Although delicious, is definitely one kept for special occasions due to the fat content of double cream. Nevertheless, the SuperFood salmon provides a valuable source of vitamin D, high-quality protein and omega 3 fatty acids for the entire family.

400g (14oz) linguine

50ml (2fl oz) olive oil

1 onion - peeled, chopped

2 tsp minced garlic

1 tsp ground paprika

½ tsp ground nutmeg

¼ tsp ground black pepper

300ml (½ pint) double cream

4 x 120g (4oz) salmon fillets (skinless, boneless) – cubed

120g (4oz) peas - frozen, washed

Salt to taste (optional)

Ground cayenne pepper to taste (optional)

Fresh flat leaf parsley for garnish - washed, chopped

Cook the linguine according to packet instructions.

Heat the oil in a pot, add the onion and stir-fry until golden. Add garlic, paprika, nutmeg, black pepper and stir-fry for 30secs then pour in the double cream, add the salmon and simmer covered for 5-6mins on low heat until the salmon chunks are flaky and break apart easily.

Whilst the sauce is simmering, steam the peas in a steamer or in the microwave by placing them in a microwavable dish and adding 2 tablespoons of water. Cover the dish with either a lid (leaving a small vent) or cling film (piercing a few holes), and steam on high for 1-1½mins until tender. Once cooked, drain the excess water and add to the sauce at the end. Combine well.

Remove a serving for your little one and set aside. Add salt and cayenne pepper to the main pot and stir. Return to the heat for a further 1-2mins then garnish the main serving (and your little ones) with parsley. Serve warm.

IMPORTANT: ensure there are no fish bones included within baby's serving.

Masala Fish Curry

A gorgeous, tangy fish curry with a hint of fire (for the adults). For your little one, this is an excellent way to get some tasty fish into her diet. The lemon acts as a wonderful substitute to salt by providing a sharp taste to the fish and combined with the tomatoes, is a superb source of antioxidant vitamin C. The fish is also a great source of protein and B vitamins.

Marinade:

3 tbsp olive oil

1 tbsp tomato puree

1 tsp ground coriander

1 tsp ground cumin

1 tsp minced garlic

½ tsp ground turmeric

½ lemon — freshly squeezed

Salt to taste (optional)

4 x 100g (3½oz) white fish fillets (skinless, boneless)

Sauce:

3 tbsp olive oil

200g (7oz) tinned chopped tomatoes

Salt to taste (optional)

Red chilli powder to taste (optional)

Fresh coriander/ cilantro for garnish — washed

Marinade: Place the oil, tomato puree, coriander, cumin, garlic, turmeric, lemon juice in a bowl and combine. Remove one tablespoon of marinade and set aside – this will be used for the curry sauce later. Then cover one fish fillet (for toddler) with the marinade and also set aside. Add salt to the remaining marinade and cover the remaining fillets. Set aside for 30mins.

Sauce: Heat the oil in a large frying pan, add the tomatoes and the 'saved' tablespoon of marinade. Simmer until the sauce thickens, then add the marinated fish fillets to the pan. Continue to simmer for 6-8mins or until the fish is flaky. Turn over halfway. Once cooked, remove toddler's fish fillet and some curry sauce and set aside. Then add salt and red chilli powder to the pan and return to the heat for a further 1-2mins. Garnish the main serving (and your little ones) with fresh coriander/ cilantro and serve with roti or rice and alongside my delicious Tarka Coconut Dhal (page 149).

IMPORTANT: ensure there are no fish bones included within baby's serving.

Quick Kids SuperMeals

These days Aaliyah is attending preschool and when she comes home she's ravenous from all the running around and playing she's been doing with her friends. She needs some grub quickly to refuel, and I need to give her some grub quickly to stop the whining. So my focus on her meals has shifted slightly. Nutrition is still my number one priority when it comes to her diet, but now I find myself looking for quick and easy snacks to feed her between meals. These **'booster' snacks** take no longer than 15 minutes to prepare, they are ALL still nutritional SuperMeals, and they are simple – **fuss-free!**

I have to say these meals really are handy, having been both a stay-at-home mum and a working mum, I can honestly say I was always **struggling for time** regardless of whether I was at home looking after Aaliyah and trying to get the never-ending house work finished; or I was at work, coming home and still trying to get the never-ending house work finished! So with the lack of time being a major factor in people's lives, these recipes are perfect for whipping up healthy, nutritious meals or snacks in minutes. And are extremely handy for famished kids after school.

Quick Cook Foods in Each Food Group

	Pasta	10-12mins
	White basmati rice	10mins
Carb-Rich (starches)	Cous Cous	10mins
	Roti/ chappati	ready-made, instant use
	Pitta	ready-made, instant use
	Bread (white and brown)	ready-made, instant use
Milk and Dairy	Cheese, milk, yogurt	ready-made, instant use
	Chicken breast fillet	15-20mins
Protein-Rich	Fish fillet	5-8mins
	Eggs	3-5mins
Vegetables	Various	between 2-10mins to steam. Some take longer than others
Fruits	Various	ready for instant use - just requires a little chopping time

Quick Meal Cooking Techniques

The Microwave is Your Friend: Speed up the cooking process by changing your cooking technique. For example, instead of boiling potatoes which can take 15 minutes - sometimes longer, steam them in the microwave from anywhere between 3-6 minutes (depending on their size), and reduce cooking time by more than half. Alternatively cook them using a steamer if you have one. Either way both methods will help to maintain valuable nutrients in vegetables and will save you time.

Multi-task: Multi-tasking might seem like very obvious thing to do but it's very easy to be so focussed on cooking one part of a meal, that you can forget the other part. When I first started cooking I'd concentrate on getting the curry right first, and after it was bubbling away, I'd put the rice on the stove to cook. It's only after I started cooking both at the same time (after I had Aaliyah), that multi-tasking saved me about 10-15mins. This meant, we were eating dinner earlier, which meant Aaliyah was getting ready for bed earlier, which meant a little more relaxing time after she was in bed in the evenings.

Super Quick Bombay Potatoes

Bombay potatoes are a popular delicious snack or accompaniment to a larger family meal. Bursting with white SuperFoods – garlic and potato, this snack is high in antioxidant activity. The potato is carb-rich - great for energy, and is potassium-rich, necessary for heart function and the function of all other internal organs. Mustard seeds are also antioxidant and rich in selenium, an anti-cancer mineral also found in chicken.

Place the potato cubes in a pot, cover with water, bring to the boil and simmer for 15mins until tender. Drain and set aside.

Alternatively, save time and steam them in a steamer or in the microwave by placing them in a microwavable dish and adding 2 tablespoons of water. Cover the dish with either a lid (leaving a small vent) or cling film (piercing a few holes), and steam on high for 3-4mins until tender. Once cooked, drain and set aside.

Whilst the potatoes are cooking, heat the oil in a non-stick frying pan on medium-low heat and add the mustard seeds. When they begin to sizzle and pop, turn to low heat and add the garlic, ginger and stir-fry for a few seconds. Then immediately add a splash of water (be careful of the sprays and sizzles), the tomato puree and stir-fry until the tomato puree and water combine to form a masala sauce.

Finally add the cooked potato cubes to the frying pan and combine with the masala. Cook for a further few seconds and remove from the heat. Serve warm.

1 white potato – washed, peeled, cut into 1" cubes

½ tbsp olive oil

¼ tsp brown mustard seeds

¼ tsp minced garlic

¼ tsp minced ginger

1 tbsp tomato puree

Indian Salad Roti Wrap

I love Sambharo - a warm Indian salad prepared using SuperFoods cabbage and carrots sautéed in a few spices and steamed until soft. And due to its uncomplicated nature is a quick accompaniment to any Indian meal. This is a carb-rich snack (courtesy of the roti) which is great for providing kids with energy needed to play. Also rich in beta-carotene (carrots) and packed with white antioxidant SuperFoods (garlic and cabbage), I would highly recommend including this simple, delicious snack regularly within a child's diet.

Heat the oil in a frying pan on medium-low heat and add the mustard seeds, garlic and stir continuously until they begin to pop and sizzle. Then add the cabbage, carrots and sprinkle over the turmeric. Stir to combine well then leave to steam (covered) on low heat until the cabbage is soft; this will take between 5-7minutes.

To serve place a warm roti on a plate, spoon the sambharo in a line down the centre of the roti. Drizzle over some greek style yogurt and top with fresh coriander. Roll and cut in half for easy eating.

Repeat as necessary for up to four kids and enjoy!

Tip: If you choose to cook cabbage for any other meal, the best way to preserve the nutrients is by sautéing the cabbage.

Sambharo:

1 tbsp olive oil

1½ tsp mustard seeds

2 tsp minced garlic

Half white cabbage – washed, finely chopped

4 medium carrots – washed, peeled, shredded (using a food processor)

1 tsp ground turmeric

To serve:

1 roti – homemade or ready-made, warmed

2-3 tbsp of sambharo - warm

Dollop of greek style yogurt

Fresh coriander/ cilantro (garnish)

Baked Bean Curry

• •

Now this fabulous curry is as quick to make as it is to warm up the can of beans used to prepare it with. It is perfect served as lunch for a 3-4 year old or as an after school snack for older children. Although there is a small amount of salt within this curry, I like to counter it with the fact that baked beans are in fact... SUPERFOODS! They are loaded with protein, necessary for healthy growth, fibre-rich, and the tomato sauce they are covered in is a source of lycopene which is antioxidant and anti-cancer.

½ tbsp olive oil

½ tsp minced garlic

½ tsp mustard seeds

½ tsp cumin seeds

1 x 200g (7oz) can of baked beans – low salt/ low sugar variety

Pinch of ground ginger

¼ tsp ground coriander

Pinch of ground turmeric

Pinch of ground black pepper

Heat the oil in a small pot on low heat and add garlic, mustard seeds and cumin. Stir-fry continuously for 2 minutes allowing them to sizzle for a while then add the baked beans and stir.

Add the ginger, coriander, turmeric and black pepper, stir and simmer for 5 minutes on low heat and it's done! Remove from the heat and set aside.

Serve alongside some warm buttery granary toast for my twist on British classic - beans on toast. Alternatively serve with a jacket potato for a more filling meal.

Tip: Keep your child's daily salt in-take low by creating two servings from this curry reducing the salt content by half.

Mini Masala Omelettes

• •

I like to call these little gems protein-rich pancakes! Excellent for healthy growth, delicious, and the teeny weeny size makes them very appealing to kids. Add a few aromatic spices for extra flavour and this one will become a firm after school favourite.

1 egg

¼ small onion – peeled, finely chopped

2 baby plum tomatoes (or ¼ regular tomato) – washed, chopped

Pinch of ground black pepper

Pinch of ground garam masala

Pinch of ground cumin

3-4 fresh coriander leaves – washed, finely chopped

Salt (optional)

1 tsp olive oil

Crack the egg into a bowl and add the onion, tomatoes, black pepper, garam masala, cumin, coriander leaves and salt (if you wish), and whisk the whole lot together.

Pour the oil into a small non-stick frying pan, heat the oil and add half of the egg mixture. Cook on medium-low heat for a few minutes until the top is no longer runny, turn it over and cook on the other side for another minute or two. Remove from the heat and repeat for the second omelette. Serve with roti or with warm buttered toast and a side of salad.

Tip: If you don't have a small frying pan to make mini omelettes, make one large one instead.

Fragrant Sweet Pepper Pilaf

The fragrance in this snack comes from the gorgeous whole garam masalas the rice is cooked with – cinnamon, cloves and cardamom. Extremely quick to cook, this is hassle-free one pot meal which will provide your little one with an extra oomph before dinner.

Heat the oil in a pot, add the onion and stir-fry until soft and golden. Add the garlic, stir-fry for a minute and add the rice, water, salt and stir. Bring to the boil and simmer (covered) for 10mins until the rice is tender. Switch off the hob and allow the rice to continue to steam for a further 2-3mins (covered).

Once finished, fluff the rice with a fork, add the peppers for a sweet crunch, combine well with the rice and serve with a side salad.

Tip: serve this rice as an accompaniment to evening meals for a twist on your everyday rice.

IMPORTANT: ensure all whole garam masalas are removed from the pot before serving.

50ml (2fl oz) olive oil

1 onion – peeled, chopped

1 cinnamon stick

2 whole cloves

2 cardamom pods- green

200g (7oz) white basmati rice

1½ tsp minced garlic

375ml (12¼fl oz) of water

Salt to taste

1 red or yellow bell pepper – washed, deseeded, diced

APPENDIX I - Food Storage Guidelines

Food type	Preparation	Freezing	Refrigerating	Heating
Curries	Cook 2-3 different curries at a time - one protein/ one veggie to ensure a balanced diet. Allow cooling and prepare individual servings (see appendix II).	Ensure your freezer is set to 0F (-18C) or below, and curries will keep for 6-8 weeks.	Store in the fridge for up to 48 hours.	From frozen - thaw in the fridge/ microwave. Heat until piping hot, then allowing cooling before serving. From chilled - heat until piping hot, then allowing cooling before serving. Important: ALWAYS test the temperature to ensure there are no hotspots.
Pitta bread (ready-made)	N/A	Freeze on day of purchase. Will keep for 6-8 weeks.	Once packet opened, will last for up to 72 hours. Sometimes longer.	From frozen - thaw in the fridge, microwave or toaster. Heat until piping hot, then allowing cooling before serving. From chilled - heat in the microwave, oven, grill or toaster. Allow cooling before serving.
Quinoa	Allow cooked quinoa to cool and prepare immediately into individual servings (see appendix II)	Ensure your freezer is set to 0F (-18C) or below, and quinoa will keep for 6-8 weeks.	Store in the fridge for up to 48 hours.	From frozen - thaw in the fridge/ microwave. Heat until piping hot, then allowing cooling before serving. From chilled - heat until piping hot, then allowing cooling before serving. Important: ALWAYS test the temperature to ensure there are no hotspots.
Rice	Lay freshly cooked rice flat on a tray and allow to cool, then prepare individual servings (see appendix II), and immediately place in the fridge/ freezer to avoid bacterial growth when the rice is at room temperature.	Ensure your freezer is set to 0F (-18C) or below, and rice will keep for 6-8 weeks.	Store in the fridge for up to 48 hours.	From frozen - thaw in the fridge/ microwave. Heat until piping hot, then allowing cooling before serving. From chilled - heat until piping hot, then allowing cooling before serving. Important: ALWAYS test the temperature to ensure there are no hotspots.
Roti (home-made)	Lay freshly cooked rotis flat on the counter or on a tray and allow cooling. Then collect in a pile, wrap in foil and place in a large freezer bag and seal.	Ensure your freezer is set to 0F (-18C) or below, and one batch of rotis will keep for 6-8 weeks. Note: one frozen roti pulls apart from the batch easily.	One batch will last for up to 72 hours. Sometimes longer.	From frozen - thaw in the fridge/ microwave. Heat until piping hot, then allowing cooling before serving. From chilled - heat until piping hot, then allowing cooling before serving.
Roti (ready-made)	N/A	Freeze on day of purchase. Will keep for 6-8 weeks.	Once packet opened, will last for up to 72 hours. Sometimes longer.	From frozen - thaw in the fridge/ microwave. Heat until piping hot, then allowing cooling before serving. From chilled - heat until piping hot, then allowing cooling before serving.

APPENDIX II - Individual Serving Sizes

Stages	Individual Serving Sizes
Stage 2 | 7 Months Plus	1 serving = 2 tablespoons
Stage 3 | 10 Months Plus	1 serving = 3 tablespoons

You may need to increase or reduce the amount depending on your little ones appetite.

Storage Advice

Store individual servings in good quality freezer bags, label them with the contents, date them and place them in the freezer. A flawless method of effectively rotating frozen freshly cooked food. Furthermore, freezer bags are handy for squeezing into corners if you are tight for space.

Alternatively freeze baby food in flexible ice-cube trays but ensure the tray is covered with either a lid or placed inside a freezer bag, before it is placed in the freezer; it must be clearly labelled with the contents. Once frozen, remove the baby food cubes from the tray, place them in freezer bags, label and date them, then pop them back in the freezer.

APPENDIX III - Cooking Conversion Tables and Abbreviations

Abbreviations

fl oz	fluid ounce
g	gram
lb	pound
ml	millilitre
oz	ounce
tbsp	tablespoon
tsp	teaspoon

Spoon Conversions

1 x UK teaspoon	5ml
1 x UK tablespoon	15ml (3 teaspoons)

Liquid Conversions

Metric	Imperial	Cups
50ml	2fl oz	¼ cup
120ml	4fl oz	½ cup
175ml	6fl oz	¾ cup
250ml	8fl oz	1 cup

Please note: all conversions are approximate.

Index

Resources, References and Links

Articles

Ahuja, P. 2009. **Health benefits of nutmeg.** Complete Wellbeing. [ONLINE] 16 August. Available at: http://completewellbeing.com/article/a-nutty-affair/ [Accessed 14 March 2012]

Associated Press. 2005. **Experts seek to debunk baby food myths.** msnbc.com, [ONLINE] (Last updated 10.45 PM on 09th October 2005) Available at: http://www.msnbc.msn.com/id/9646449/#. TzDvmVyRFhwU [Accessed 20 September 2011]

Associated Newspapers Ltd. 2005. **The Top 10 Super foods.** Mail Online, [ONLINE] (Last updated at 10:55 22 December 2005).Available at: http://www.dailymail.co.uk/health/article-369042/The-10-super-foods.html [Accessed 8 February 2012]

Bennett, Coleman and Co. 2012. **Use herbs, spices to keep cold at bay.** The Times of India, [ONLINE] 9 January. Available at:http://articles.timesofindia.indiatimes.com/2012-01-09/kanpur/30607134_1_indian-spice-winter-ailments-cloves [Accessed 11 January 2012]

Bond, AB. 2005. **Top 12 Superfood Herbs and Spices.** Care2, [ONLINE] 30 March. Available at: http://www.care2.com/greenliving/top-12-superfood-herbs-and-spice.html#ixzz1jStivjXK [Accessed 18 January 2012]

Cespedes, A. 2010. **Worcestershire Sauce Nutrition.** Livestrong.com, [ONLINE] 31 December. Available at: http://www.livestrong.com/article/346527-worcestershire-sauce-nutrition/ [Accessed 17 April 2012]

Ericson, J. 2014. **Oregano Oil Fights Norovirus: Carvacrol Shown to Kill Foodborne Pathogen, Hints At New Disinfectant.** Medical Daily. [ONLINE] 11 February. Available at: http://www.medicaldaily. com/oregano-oil-fights-norovirus-carvacrol-shown-kill-foodborne-pathogen-hints-new-disinfectant-269123 [Accessed 17 March 2014]

Evans, K. 2011. **Flavonoids in fruits, vegetables and nuts dramatically lower cancer rates.** Natural News.com, [ONLINE] 28 September. Available at: http://www.naturalnews.com/033708_cancer_flavonoids.html [Accessed 7 December 2011]

Gasior, K. 2011. **The Benefits of Paprika.** Livestrong.com [ONLINE] (Last updated on 8th September 2011). Available at: http://www.livestrong.com/article/539058-the-benefits-of-paprika/ [Accessed 31 March 2012]

Hari, S, M.D. 1995. **Free Radicals: A Major Cause of Aging and Disease.** Consumer Health, [ONLINE] Available at: http://www.consumerhealth.org/articles/display.cfm?ID=19990303172533 [Accessed 8 March 2012]

Jockers, D, Dr. 2010. **Discover the Superfood power of coconut.** Natural News.com [ONLINE] 25 September. Available at: http://www.naturalnews.com/029841_coconut_superfood.html [Accessed 19 October 2011]

Kassem, N. 2011. **Nutritional content of Honey.** Livestrong.com [ONLINE] 10 February. Available at: http://www.livestrong.com/article/378810-nutritional-content-of-honey/ [Accessed 30 April 2012]

Keefer, A. 2011. **Calcium Absorption and Potassium.** Livestrong.com [ONLINE] 1 September. Available at: http://www.livestrong.com/article/528043-calcium-absorption-potassium/ [Accessed 19 December 2011]

Kellow, J, BSc RD. 2000. **From Snack Foods to Superfoods - Pop Corn and Whole Grain Cereals.** Weight Loss Resources, [ONLINE] Available at: http://www.weightlossresources.co.uk/food/healthy/superfoods/pop-corn-whole-grain-breakfast-cereals.htm [Accessed 22 March 2012]

Kovacs, B, MS, RD. 2012. **Probiotics.** MedicineNet.com [ONLINE] Available at: http://www.medicinenet.com/probiotics/article.htm [Accessed 7 March 2012]

Laurance, J. 2007. **The Big Question. What are Superfoods and are they really so good for our health?** The Independent, [ONLINE] 16 February. Available at: http://www.independent.co.uk/life-style/health-and-families/health-news/the-big-question-what-are-superfoods-and-are-they-really-so-good-for-our-health-436529.html [Accessed 3 February 2012]

Magee, E, MPH, RD. 2007. **The Super-Veggies: Cruciferous Vegetables.** WebMD, [ONLINE] 19 April. Available at: http://www.webmd.com/food-recipes/features/super-veggies-cruciferous-vegetables [Accessed 6 March 12]

Maternowski, T. 2011. **Does Eating Pepper affect the unborn baby?** Livestrong.com, [ONLINE] 28 March. Available at:http://www.livestrong.com/article/258605-does-eating-pepper-affect-the-unborn-baby/ [Accessed 12 October 2011]

MedicalDaily.com. 2010. **Health benefits of Mangoes.** Medical Daily [ONLINE] 7 November. Available at: http://www.medicaldaily.com/news/20101107/3414/health-benefits-of-mangoes.htm [Accessed 14 March 2012]

MediLexicon International Ltd. 2009. **Common Food Allergies.** Medical News Today, [ONLINE] 12 May. Available at: http://www.medicalnewstoday.com/releases/8624.php [Accessed 16 September 2011]

MediLexicon International Ltd. 2009. **Oleocanthal May Help Prevent, Treat Alzheimer's.** Medical News Today, [ONLINE] 30 September. Available at: http://www.medicalnewstoday.com/releases/165611.php [Accessed 9 February 2012]

MediLexicon International Ltd. 2004. **What are Proteins?** Medical News Today, [ONLINE] 23 September. Available at: http://www.medicalnewstoday.com/releases/13903.php [Accessed 26 January 2012]

Nakauchi, L. 2011. **Lady Finger herb provides colon health.** Natural News.com [ONLINE] 8 October. Available at: http://www.naturalnews.com/033807_colon_health_lady_finger.html [Accessed 2 May 2012]

Phillip, J. 2011. **Black raspberries and anthocyanin's demonstrate powerful cancer fighting power.** Natural News.com [ONLINE] 14 April. Available at: http://www.naturalnews.com/032068_black_raspberries_cancer.html [Accessed 16 February 2012]

Roberts, M. 2012. **Spoon Feeding 'makes babies fatter'.** BBC News Health, [ONLINE] (Last updated 01:48 on 7th February 2012). Available at: http://www.bbc.co.uk/news/health-16905371 [Accessed 10 February 2012]

Sample, I. 2008. **Health: Breastfed babies more receptive to tastes, say food research scientists.** The Guardian, [ONLINE] 24 July. Available at: http://www.guardian.co.uk/science/2008/jul/24/humanbehaviour.foodtech [Accessed 30 September 2011]

ScienceDaily LLC. 2005. **Raisins As A Functional Food for Oral Health.** ScienceDaily, [ONLINE] 13 June. Available at: http://www.sciencedaily.com/releases/2005/06/050613062724.htm [Accessed 13 March 2012]

Selke, LA. 2010. **What kind of spices can I use in my baby's food?** Livestrong.com, [ONLINE] 2 September. Available at:http://www.livestrong.com/article/218627-what-kind-of-spices-can-i-use-in-my-babys-food/ [Accessed 17 September 2011]

Telegraph Media Group Ltd. 2011. **Health benefits of Vitamin D.** The Telegraph. [ONLINE] 12 April. Available at: http://www.telegraph.co.uk/health/healthnews/8444739/Health-benefits-of-vitamin-D.html [Accessed 12 October 2011]

Uher, P. 2010. **Health benefits of cardamom.** Helium, [ONLINE] 4 March. Available at: http://www.helium.com/items/1761448-what-are-the-health-benefits-of-the-spice-cardamom [Accessed 21 March 2012]

University of Maryland Medical Center. 2011. **Manganese.** [ONLINE] (Last updated on 10th July 2011). Available at: http://www.umm.edu/altmed/articles/manganese-000314.htm [Accessed 31 January 2012]

University of Maryland Medical Center. 2011. **Omega-3 fatty acids.** [ONLINE] (Last updated on 10th May 2011).Available at: http://www.umm.edu/altmed/articles/omega-3-000316.htm [Accessed 7 March 2012]

Vandermark, T. 2011. **The nutritional benefits of eggplant.** Livestrong.com, [ONLINE] (Last updated on 26th April 2011). Available at: http://www.livestrong.com/article/19046-nutritional-benefits-eggplant/ [Accessed 28 September 2011]

Vandermark, T. 2011. **What is the nutritional value of dates?** Livestrong.com, [ONLINE] (Last updated on 26th April 2011. Available at: http://www.livestrong.com/article/17923-nutritional-value-dates/ [Accessed 13 March 2012]

Walling, E. 2009. **Learn About the Many Benefits of Lauric Acid in Coconut oil.** Natural News.com [ONLINE] 11 August. Available at: http://www.naturalnews.com/026819_lauric_acid_coconut_oil_infections.html [Accessed 19 October 2011]

Zelman, K, MPH, RD/LD. 2008. **The Benefits of Vitamin C.** MedicineNet.com, [ONLINE] 4 April. Available at: http://www.medicinenet.com/script/main/art.asp?articlekey=88519 [Accessed 6 March 2012]

Books and Journals

Chaturvedi TP. 2009. **Uses of turmeric in dentistry: An update.** Indian J Dent Res. [E-JOURNAL] 20 (1): 107-109. Available at:http://www.ijdr.in/text.asp?2009/20/1/107/49065 [Accessed 4 October 2011]

Department of Health. 2009. **NHS Birth to Five.** London: Produced by COI

Dewanto, V, Wu, X and Liu, RH. 2002. **Processed Sweet Corn has Higher Antioxidant Activity.** J. Agric. Food Chem. [E-JOURNAL] 50 (17) 4959 —4964. Abstract only. Available at: http://pubs.acs.org/doi/abs/10.1021/jf0255937 [Accessed 10 February 2012]

Jagetia GC and Aggarwal BB. 2007. **"Spicing up" of the immune system by curcumin.** J Clin Immunol. [E-JOURNAL] 27 (1): 19-35. Available at:http://www.curcuminresearch.org/PDF/Jagetia%20GC-21.pdf [Accessed 2 October 2011]

Karmel, A. 2001. **Annabel Karmel's Superfoods for Babies and Children.** London: Ebury Press.

Mennella JA, PhD, Jagnow CP and Beauchamp GK, PhD. (2001) **Prenatal and Postnatal Flavor Learning by Human Infants.** Pediatrics. [E-JOURNAL] 107 (6): E88. Available at:http://www.ncbi.nlm.nih.gov/pmc/articles/PMC1351272/pdf/nihms-5608.pdf [Accessed 28 September 2011]

Rajeshwari U and Andallu B. 2011. **Medicinal benefits of coriander (Coriandrum Sativum L).**Spatula DD. [E-JOURNAL] 1 (1), 51-58. Available at:http://www.scopemed.org/fulltextpdf.php?mno=2633 [Accessed 26 October 2011]

Shobana, K and Naidu, A. 2000. **Antioxidant activity of selected Indian spices.** PLEFA. [E-JOURNAL] 62 (2), 107-110. Abstract only. Available at: http://www.sciencedirect.com/science/article/pii/S095232789990128X [Accessed 7 November 2011]

Skulas-Ray et al. 2011. **A high antioxidant spice blend attenuates postprandial insulin and triglyceride responses and increases some plasma measures of antioxidant activity in healthy, overweight men.** J Nutr. [E-JOURNAL] 10, 3945. 1-7. Available at: http://jn.nutrition.org/content/early/2011/06/22/jn.111.138966.full.pdf [Accessed 10 January 2012]

Sommerburg O, Keunen JEE, Bird AC and Van Kuijk FJGM. 1998. **Fruits and vegetables that are sources for lutein and zeaxanthin: the macular pigment in human eyes.** Br J Ophthalmol. [E-JOURNAL] 82, 907-910. Available at: http://www.ncbi.nlm.nih.gov/pmc/articles/PMC1722697/pdf/v082p00907.pdf [Accessed 7 December 2011]

Fact Sheets

Condé Nast. 2012. **Self-Nutrition Data -Cream, fluid, heavy whipping.** [ONLINE] Available at: http://nutritiondata.self.com/facts/dairy-and-egg-products/51/2 [Accessed 8 May 2012]

Department of Health. 2011. NHS **Introducing Solid Foods. Giving your baby a better start in life.** [PDF] Available at: http://www.dh.gov.uk/prod_consum_dh/groups/dh_digitalassets/documents/digitalasset/dh_125828.pdf [Accessed 22 November 2011]

Food — a fact of life. 2009. **Estimated average requirements (EARS) for Energy.** [ONLINE] Available at: http://www.google.co.uk/url?sa=tandrct=jandq=andesrc=sandsource=webandcd=1andsqi=2andved=0CFQQFjAAandurl=http%3A%2F%2Fwww.foodafactoflife.org.uk%2Fattachments%2Fbff0c546-9cf1-485db51d1cf2.docandei=K8D2T82tNumY0QXniKiIBwandusg=AFQjCNErLbXck47XLYYuWYlw_1uI-ujBBA [Accessed 6 March 2012]

Nutrition-and-you.com. 2010. **Cardamom nutrition facts.** [ONLINE]- Available at: http://www.nutrition-and-you.com/cardamom.html [Accessed 5 March 2012]

Office of Dietary Supplements - National Institutes of Health. 2009. **Folate.** [ONLINE] (Last reviewed on 15th April 2009). Available at: http://ods.od.nih.gov/factsheets/folate/ [Accessed 7 March 2012]

Office of Dietary Supplements - National Institutes of Health. 2011. **Selenium.** [ONLINE] (Last reviewed 11th October 2011). Available at: http://ods.od.nih.gov/factsheets/Selenium-HealthProfessional/ [Accessed 20 February 2012]

Office of Dietary Supplements - National Institutes of Health. 2011. **Zinc.** [ONLINE] (Last reviewed on 20th September 2011). Available at: http://ods.od.nih.gov/factsheets/Zinc-HealthProfessional/ [Accessed 24 February 2012]

Reports

Foods Standards Agency. 2001. **Expert Group on Vitamins and Minerals - Revised Review of Vitamin C.** [ONLINE] Available at: http://www.food.gov.uk/multimedia/pdfs/vitaminc.pdf [Accessed 5 January 2012]

Health & Social Care Information Centre. 2013. **National Child Measurement Programme: England, 2012/ 13 School Year.** [ONLINE] Available at: http://www.hscic.gov.uk/catalogue/PUB13115/nati-chil-meas-prog-eng-2012-2013-rep.pdf [Accessed 1 January 2014]

U.S. Department of Agriculture. 2009. **National Nutrient Database for Standard Reference, Release 22. Lycopene (µg) Content of Selected Foods per Common Measure, sorted by nutrient content.** [ONLINE] Available at: http://www.ars.usda.gov/SP2UserFiles/Place/12354500/Data/SR22/nutrlist/sr22w337.pdf [Accessed 9 December 2011]

U.S. Department of Agriculture. 2010. **USDA Database for the Oxygen Radical Absorbance Capacity (ORAC) of Selected Foods, Release 2.** [ONLINE] Available at:http://www.orac-info-portal.de/download/ORAC_R2.pdf [Accessed 18 October 2011]

Websites

American Cancer Society. 2008. **Ellagic Acid. Find Support and Treatment.** [ONLINE] (Last updated on 1st November 2008). Available at: http://www.cancer.org/Treatment/TreatmentsandSideEffects/ComplementaryandAlternativeMedicine/DietandNutrition/ellagic-acid [Accessed 6 February 2012]

American Cancer Society. 2010. **Lycopene. Find Support and Treatment.** [ONLINE] (Last updated on 13th May 2011). Available at: http://www.cancer.org/Treatment/TreatmentsandSideEffects/ComplementaryandAlternativeMedicine/DietandNutrition/lycopene [Accessed 6 February 2012]

AntioxidantsDetective.com. 2009. **The Benefits of Selenium.** [ONLINE] Available at: http://www.antioxidantsdetective.com/benefits-of-selenium.html [Accessed 15 February 2012]

Antioxidants-for-Health-and-Longevity.com. 2009. **Cumin Health Benefits Come from Antioxidants.** [ONLINE] Available at: http://www.antioxidants-for-health-and-longevity.com/cumin-health-benefits.html [Accessed 11 January 2012]

Antioxidants-for-health-and-longevity.com. 2009. **Health Benefits of Cloves Nature's Top Antioxidant Food.** [ONLINE] Available at: http://www.antioxidants-for-health-and-longevity.com/benefits-of-cloves.html [Accessed 11 January 2012]

Baby Centre. 2009. **Food Allergies.** [ONLINE] Available at: http://www.babycentre.co.uk/baby/startingsolids/foodallergies/ [Accessed 18 August 2011]

Baby Center India. 2008. **When and how should I add spices in my baby's food?** [ONLINE] Available at: http://www.babycenter.in/baby/startingsolids/spicesinbabyfoodexpert/ [Accessed 17 September 2011]

BBC Health. 2012. **Weaning.** [ONLINE] Available at: http://www.bbc.co.uk/health/physical_health/child_development/babies_weaning.shtml [Accessed 2 January 2012]

Christine. 2009. **The Goodness of Garlic for Baby.** Home Made Baby Food Recipes Blog [BLOG] 6 November. Available at: http://blog.homemade-baby-food-recipes.com/the-goodness-of-garlic-for-baby/ [Accessed 19 September 2011]

Christine. 2009. **Why Turmeric Is One of The Best Spices You Can Give Your Baby.** Home Made Baby Food Recipes Blog [BLOG] 10 September. Available at: http://blog.homemade-baby-food-recipes.com/why-turmeric-is-one-of-the-best-spices-you-can-give-your-baby/ [Accessed 19 September 2011]

Coconut Research Centre. 2004. **Coconut.** [ONLINE] Available at: http://www.coconutresearchcenter.org/ [Accessed 19 October 2011]

Condon, S. 1997. **Is it okay to eat spicy food while nursing?** Baby Centre [ONLINE] Available at:http://www.babycenter.com/404_is-it-okay-to-eat-spicy-food-while-nursing_1931.bc [Accessed 6 September 2011]

Garden-Robinson, J, Ph.D., L.R.D. 2011. **What Color is your food? Taste a rainbow of fruit and vegetables for better health.** North Dakota State University [ONLINE] (Last reviewed May 2011). Available at: http://www.ag.ndsu.edu/pubs/yf/foods/fn595w.htm [Accessed 5 February 2012]

Healthaliciousness.com. 2008. **Top 10 Foods Highest in Beta Carotene.** [ONLINE] Available at: http://www.healthaliciousness.com/articles/natural-food-sources-of-beta-carotene.php [Accessed 29 February 2012]

Healthaliciousness.com. 2008. **Top 10 Foods Highest in Lycopene.** [ONLINE] Available at: http://www.healthaliciousness.com/articles/high-lycopene-foods.php. [Accessed 29 February 2012]

Healthaliciousness.com. 2008. **Top 10 Foods Highest in Vitamin A.** [ONLINE] Available at: http://www.healthaliciousness.com/articles/food-sources-of-vitamin-A.php[Accessed 29 February 2012]

Health Diaries. 2010. **Eat This! - 6 Health Benefits of Lentils.** [ONLINE] 7 November. Available at: http://www.healthdiaries.com/eatthis/6-health-benefits-of-lentils.html [Accessed 20 December 2011]

Homemade Baby Food Recipes. 2011. **Can Babies Eat Spicy Food?** [ONLINE] (Last updated on 1st June 2011). Available at: http://www.homemade-baby-food-recipes.com/can-babies-eat-spicy-food.html [Accessed 19 September 2011]

Home Remedies Web.com. 2006. **Cinnamon Health Benefits.** [ONLINE] Available at: http://www.homeremediesweb.com/cinnamon_health_benefits.php [Accessed 11 November 2011]

Hood, KJM. 2011. **Paneer cheese and its health benefits!** Sjogren's Syndrome Blog. [ONLINE] 12 October. Available at: http://sjogrensblog.org/2011/10/12/paneer-cheese-and-its-health-benefits/ [Accessed 26 April 2012]

Iovinelli, BM, RN, BSN, IBCLC. 2011. **When can babies have spices in their food?** Baby Zone [ONLINE] Available at: http://www.babyzone.com/askanexpert/baby-spices-solid-food [Accessed 19 September 2011]

Lycopene benefits.org. 2012. **Lycopene benefits.**[ONLINE] Available at: http://lycopenebenefits.org/ [Accessed 6 February 2012]

McCormick Science Institute. 2009. **Spices, Herbs and Antioxidants.** [ONLINE] Available at: http://www.mccormickscienceinstitute.com/content.cfm?ID=10437 [Accessed 22 October 2011]

MedlinePlus. 2011. **B Vitamins.** [ONLINE] Available at: http://www.nlm.nih.gov/medlineplus/bvitamins.html [Accessed 6 March 2012]

MedlinePlus. 2010. **Potassium in diet.** [ONLINE] Available at: http://www.nlm.nih.gov/medlineplus/ency/article/002413.htm [Accessed 19 December 2011]

Miller, D. 2008. **Color Wheel of Fruits and Vegetables.** Disabled World [ONLINE] 12 January. Available at: http://www.disabled-world.com/artman/publish/fruits-vegetables.shtml [Accessed 5 February 2012]

Momtastic's Wholesome Baby Food. 2011. **Spice Up Your Baby's World - Learn about adding Spices and Herbs to Baby's Homemade Baby Foods.** [ONLINE] (Last updated on 26th July 2011). Available at: http://wholesomebabyfood.momtastic.com/tipspices.htm [Accessed 19 September 2011]

Natural Health Cure. 2011. **Health Benefits of Saffron.** [ONLINE] 2 March. Available at: http://www.naturalhealthcure.org/healing-medicinal-herbs/health-benefits-of-saffron-uses.html [Accessed 4 March 2012]

NHS Choices. 2011. **5 A DAY portion sizes.** [ONLINE] (Last reviewed on 6th December 2011). Available at: http://www.nhs.uk/Livewell/5ADAY/Pages/Portionsizes.aspx [Accessed 21 April 2012]

NHS Choices. **Milk and dairy foods.** [ONLINE] (Last reviewed on 15th March 2011). Available at: http://www.nhs.uk/livewell/goodfood/pages/milk-dairy-foods.aspx [Accessed 6 March 2012]

NHS Choices. 2011. **Understanding Food Groups.** [ONLINE] (Last reviewed on 29th July 2011). Available at: http://www.nhs.uk/Planners/birthtofive/Pages/Thefoodgroupsexplained.aspx [Accessed 16 March 2012]

NHS Choices. 2011. **Vitamins and minerals - B vitamins and folic acid.** [ONLINE] (Last reviewed on 14th March 2011). Available at: http://www.nhs.uk/Conditions/vitamins-minerals/Pages/Vitamin-B.aspx [Accessed 6 March 2012]

NHS Choices. 2011. **Vitamins and Minerals - Vitamin A.** [ONLINE] (Last reviewed on 14th March 2011) Available at: http://www.nhs.uk/CONDITIONS/VITAMINS-MINERALS/Pages/Vitamin-A.aspx [Accessed 6 March 2012]

NHS Choices. 2011. **Vitamins and Minerals - Vitamin K.** [ONLINE] (Last reviewed on 14th March 2011). Available at: http://www.nhs.uk/Conditions/vitamins-minerals/Pages/Vitamin-K.aspx [Accessed 7 March 2012]

NHS Choices. 2011. **Your baby's first solid foods.** [ONLINE] (Last reviewed on 19th April 2011). Available at: http://www.nhs.uk/Conditions/pregnancy-and-baby/Pages/solid-foods-weaning.aspx [Accessed 13 August 2011]

Nutritional Supplements Centre. 2005. **Vitamin E.** [ONLINE] Available at: http://www.nutritionalsupplementscenter.com/info/vitamins/vitamine.html [Accessed 8 February 2012]

Schenker, S. 2010. **I've heard some babies are allergic to fruit. Which fruits may be a problem?** Baby Centre, [ONLINE] Available at:http://www.babycentre.co.uk/baby/startingsolids/safety/fruit-allergy/ [Accessed 18 September 2011]

Teens Health. 2012. **Thyroid Disease and Teens.** [ONLINE] (Last reviewed February 2012). Available at: http://kidshealth.org/teen/diseases_conditions/growth/thyroid.html# [Accessed 4 March 2012]

The George Mateljan Foundation. 2001. **The World's Healthiest Foods - Avocados.** [ONLINE] Available at: http://www.whfoods.com/genpage.php?tname=foodspiceanddbid=5 [Accessed 24 November 2011]

The George Mateljan Foundation. 2001. **The World's Healthiest Foods -Cumin Seeds.** [ONLINE] Available at:http://www.whfoods.com/genpage.php?tname=foodspiceanddbid=91. [Accessed 11 January 2012]

The George Mateljan Foundation. 2001. **The World's Healthiest Foods - Garbanzo Beans.** [ONLINE] Available at: http://www.whfoods.com/genpage.php?tname=foodspiceanddbid=58 [Accessed 16 April 2012]

The George Mateljan Foundation. 2001. **The World's Healthiest Foods - Green Beans.** [ONLINE] Available at: http://www.whfoods.com/genpage.php?tname=foodspiceanddbid=134 [Accessed 30 September 2011]

The George Mateljan Foundation. 2001. **The World's Healthiest Foods - Onions.** [ONLINE] Available at: http://whfoods.org/genpage.php?dbid=45andtname=foodspice [Accessed 6 March 2012]

The George Mateljan Foundation. 2001. **The World's Healthiest Foods - Oregano.** [ONLINE] Available at: http://www.whfoods.com/genpage.php?tname=foodspiceanddbid=73 [Accessed 26 November 2011]

The George Mateljan Foundation. 2001. **The World's Healthiest Foods - Spinach.** [ONLINE] Available at:http://whfoods.org/genpage.php?tname=foodspiceanddbid=43 [Accessed 24 November 2011]

The George Mateljan Foundation. 2001. **The World's Healthiest Foods - Turmeric.** [ONLINE] Available at: http://whfoods.org/genpage.php?tname=foodspiceanddbid=78 [Accessed 2 October 2011]

Worden, J, GP. 2011. **Carbohydrates.** Net Doctor [ONLINE] (Last updated on 12th May 2011] Available at: http://www.netdoctor.co.uk/focus/nutrition/facts/lifestylemanagement/carbohydrates.htm [Accessed 28 February 2012]

Worden, J GP. 2011. **Protein.** Net Doctor [ONLINE] (Last updated on 23rd May 2011). Available at:http://www.netdoctor.co.uk/focus/nutrition/facts/detoxification/dietaryprotein.htm [Accessed 26 January 2012]

About the Author - Zainab Jagot Ahmed

Zainab is first-time mum to daughter Aaliyah, and currently resides in Leicester, England with her husband and two cats. Prior to becoming a mummy, Zainab - a passionate home cook, worked in marketing in London for over 10 years in the fashion, entertainment and retail industries. And after the birth of her daughter, felt inspired to turn her attention to cooking nutrient-rich, homemade baby food. Zainab was keen to introduce Aaliyah to aromatic Asian flavours early when she began the weaning process, both to broaden Aaliyah's palate - allowing her to create lots of tasty meals without the use of salt or sugar, and to introduce Aaliyah to her culinary heritage. However she soon discovered there were no dedicated baby and toddler cookbooks with Asian or Asian influenced recipes. After researching aromatic spices, dietary recommendations and various SuperFoods, Zainab began inventing her own Indian-inspired baby-friendly meals, and soon friends were asking for recipes. Now she's giving everyone the chance to try them at home.

Keep up to date with the latest news and recipes from Zainab
Twitter: @ZainabJagAhmed
Facebook: facebook.com/ZainabJagotAhmed
www.ZainabJagotAhmed.com

Acknowledgments

This book would not have been possible were it not for the incredible help and team work from my amazing family and colleagues. Hubby Omar and my little bambino Aaliyah – it's finally here. The long evenings and weekend work has finally paid off. I am so very proud of this book and I hope you are too.

To my wonderful colleagues who helped make my dream into a reality – Saf, Lee, Greg, Simon and Helen. Thank you all for your help and expertise.

Special thanks to amazingly talented Claire, who has been fabulous throughout this process! I know artworking this book was a massive task and I really appreciate all the time and effort that has gone into this. This book would not have made it to the end without you.

Thank you all

Zainab xx